Come, O Blessed

&

Other Sermons

Neville Goddard

MB

DIGITALIZED BY
WATCHMAKER PUBLISHING
ALL RIGHTS RESERVED

Contents

Come, O Blessed

At times I discover that I take too much for granted. Just because I read scripture all day, I'm inclined to believe most people do - and they don't. Yesterday a doctor who has been coming here for quite a while came to see me, and I realized that I had not made myself clear; so tonight, I shall try to make this a very practical lecture, yet you will find it profoundly spiritual.

In the 25th chapter of the Book of Matthew, you will read the words: *"Come O blessed of my Father and inherit the kingdom prepared for you from the foundation of the world."* Now, this entire chapter is made up of one parable after the other. It begins with the ten wise and foolish virgins. Then the story is told of the talents and their use or misuse, followed by this statement: "I was hungry and you gave me food, thirsty and you gave me drink. I was naked and you clothed me, a stranger and you received me. I was in prison and sick and you visited me." Surprised that they are invited to inherit the kingdom prepared for them before the foundation of the world, they said to him: "When did we find you hungry and give you food, thirsty and give you drink? When did we see you as a stranger and welcome you, or naked and clothed you? And when did we see you sick and imprisoned and visited you?" And he replied: "As you did it to the least of one of these, you did it unto me."

Now, the world is looking for some external Christ, someone on the outside. Suppose right now someone in this community announces that Jesus Christ, an external being, is present. Do you know that the entire social world would turn itself over for the privilege of entertaining him? There would be quite a battle in the social world for the honor of giving him a piece of bread or a glass of water, to touch or talk to him, because they are looking for the wrong Christ. "Truly, I say to you, as you do it to one of the least of these, you do it unto me." If you had the chance to do something for Christ, wouldn't you jump at the opportunity? Well, every time you do anything to anyone in this world, you are doing it to Christ. Believe me, for he cannot come from without, as he is within you!

As William Blake said: "Awake! Awake you sleepers in the land of shadows, wake! Expand, I am in you, and you in me, mutual in love divine: I am not a God afar off, I am a brother and friend; Within your bosoms I reside, and you reside in me; Lo! We are One;" But man, not believing it, turns down the valleys dark, looking for some external God who will save him.

So, I said to my friend, the doctor: Whenever you are able to help the people who come into your office, you are serving Christ. For you see, Christ comes disguised. Sometimes he is wearing a black mask, or a white one, a yellow or a pink one and sometimes a sick one. Now, scripture makes no mention of any time when Jesus was sick, yet he makes the statement: "When I was sick you visited me." And although he does not state that he was thirsty, there is one record where he asked for a drink, and when the woman of Samaria said: "You, a Jew, talk to me, a Samarian? Jews do not talk to Samarians." Then Jesus explained the difference between the two waters saying: "If you had asked me, I would have given you living water so that you would never thirst."

Now, for the first time Jesus reveals who he really is, and it's to a woman. When she said: "I know the Messiah is coming and when he comes he will lead us into all things" he replied: "I who talk to you am he." His first revelation is to a woman, and it's to a woman that he first appears in the end. It is a bond that unfolds in this world. So, if you will do anything to anyone believing you are really doing it to Christ, you will be amazed what will happen in your world!

Now let me share with you two stories that were waiting for me when I returned from Barbados recently. This gentleman said: "A co-worker and I have lunch almost every day together. For some time he spent the entire lunch period telling me about his financial problems, and although I appeared to be interested, I really wasn't, and wondered to myself how he could possibly believe the things he was telling me. After hearing the same stories over and over again, I decided that indifference was not the answer, and I must do something about it, so in February of this year I began to listen with my inner ear. I began to hear him tell me he had more than enough money with plenty to spare.

In May he told me he came into an inheritance. He didn't say how much, but the first thing he did was to buy himself a cabin cruiser that sleeps four. Then he sent his oldest son off to college, made extensive repairs on his home, bought himself a new wardrobe and a new car. But more important to me, I discovered that my awareness has power; that indifference is not enough - I have to act!" My friend acted and "As he did it unto one of the least of these, he did it unto me." Then he said: "Every week I have my hair cut by a certain barber and even though I have moved I continued to go to his shop every Saturday, until one day it was closed. Deciding to look locally, I found a shop with four barbers and sat in the owner's chair. Each week, regardless of my request, he would not take off enough of my hair, so, having watched the other barbers, I decided to go to number four." (If you know anything about a barber shop, the number four man is the last one to arrive, and is working his way up to number one.)

"While sitting in his chair, I asked him if he liked barbering and he replied that he loved it and would love to go to an internationally recognized school for barbering. Once I discovered that he really wanted, not to be just a barber, but to be the best barber possible, I began to listen with my inner ear and heard him tell me how he graduated from the school and how much he had learned. And do you know: he not only went to the school but was the top man in his class. Then he bought out the barber, changed the personnel, and even has a receptionist to answer the phones. Now I see him every Saturday at 11:00 A.M. by appointment."

Here is a man who saw Christ in one of the least of these and clothed him in his desire, fed his desire, and gave him the living water to drink through the use of his imagination. In this world all kinds of services are needed. What if there were no barbers, only hippies and you had to cut your own hair! Suppose there were no waitresses or ladies who are willing to clean our homes! They are Christ! Each time Doris comes to clean our home, Christ walks through our door. One day she told me of a friend who had an accident. He wasn't hurt, but the car was. Then I said: "Doris, you can always buy a car, but your friend was made by God, so rejoice because he was not injured." Do you know that thought changed her completely? She attends the Catholic church, but was never told that God made her because he loved her. That he never made a thing he didn't love. Man makes cars and can replace them, but no man can replace Doris. That's how valuable she is in the eyes of God.

So here, let me give you the side benefits of praying for another. While my friend imagined these lovely things for his co-worker, his three children were named beneficiaries of an estate of a man who died in the 1890's. The estate had been in litigation for over seventy years and is only now being settled. Like Job, he prayed for his friends and his own captivity was lifted.

If I could only get you to realize that you dwell in everyone. That you are always looking at yourself pushed out! Unable to behold another, every being in the world is yourself made visible, so if you don't see the Christ in another and you are only feeding the Christ, then you do not know who "I am."

"God, Himself enters death's door with everyone who enters and lies down in the grave with him and shares his visions of eternity, until he awakes and sees Jesus and the linen clothes that the females have woven for him at the gate of the Father's house."[1] God himself, whose name is "I am" entered death's door in order for you to breathe. Being aware is saying "I am" and that's God. You will never find him in any cemetery on the outside, for God, your own wonderful human imagination, laid himself down in your skull to share your

---

[1] Wm. Blake

8

dreams of eternity until you awake. And when you do you will see the linen clothes and realize who "I am." You do not see Jesus as another, but you will know him as yourself when God's only begotten Son calls you "Father."

"I will tell you before it takes place, that when it does take place you may know that I am in my Father and you are in me and I am in you." Read this in the 14th chapter of the Book of John. Well, if I am in my Father and you are in me, then are you not in my Father? Now he tells us in the 10th chapter of John that "I and my Father are one." There is only one Father, only one body, and only one Son. There's not a bunch of little David's running around, or a bunch of little Fathers, but only the Father. So, if David calls me Father and there is only one Father, and he calls you Father, are we not the one Father? So, I tell you this before it takes place, so that when it does take place you may believe that "I am" the Father. And because you dwell in me, when it takes place in you, you will say "I am he!" In time the whole vast world will awaken to this wonderful plan and then we will have extended our creative power beyond what it was when we conceived the plan and entered death's door, this limit of contraction.

Now, I can't tell you my thrill when, in this small audience, you so believe what I tell you that you take it into the depths of your dreams as this lady did. Meeting her boyfriend's mother in dream, she was asked: "What do you think of God?" and she replied: "Christ is not external, he is within you." When you carry this truth into dream, where attention is the servant of vision and not its master, and you answer and bring it back to your surface mind, your conviction is in the very depth of your being.

Now, a chap who has been coming only recently tells me that in his dream he is trying to find someone who is very important to him. Seeing a crowd of people discussing something he sees the group separate and a young man, standing alone points toward him and says, "You are Father." Now, that's a foreshadowing. It's not the event, but a prefiguring of it. The mere fact that he saw the foreshadowing indicates that it is not far away. So, I can't tell you my thrill as I look out at this audience, for you are all awakening.

May I tell you: everything that you could possibly want is right here and ready for the taking. My friend prayed for the barber and his co-worker, as his own children became beneficiaries of an estate which had been in litigation for many years. That's the story of Job, the last chapter, the end of the journey. The unfolding of scripture could come to him suddenly, now, as it has to three of us present tonight. Having reached the end of the journey into the world of death, all of the evil that Lord had brought upon Job was removed. As we are told in the 9th chapter of John when the question was asked: "Who sinned, this man or his parents that he was born blind?" and the answer came: "Neither this man nor his parents, but that the works of the Lord be made manifest." Everything has taken place in perfect order. Even though he has not had the mystical experience of the birth from above, he has reached the end of the journey.

Now, just before I took the platform a couple came back to tell me that in a dream our friend Jan said to him: "I will not return anymore." She hasn't brought it back, but he did. In the depth, Jan told him she was not returning, and that means resurrection. In the 20th chapter of Luke, the question is asked: "Whose wife will she be in the resurrection?" and he answered: "You do not understand the scriptures. In this age they marry and are given in marriage, but those who are accounted worthy to attain to that age neither marry nor are they given in marriage, for they cannot die anymore. They are sons of God being sons of resurrection." In the depth of her soul she told that one who heard it and he brought it to the surface to share with his wife. So, I saw: the inner man is awakening, therefore it does not matter what the outer world looks like or what it does. The outer man goes on forever, for he is a part of this age of death.

But as I said earlier, who would not give their right arm to serve Jesus Christ? Don't you think that if our cardinal knew that Jesus was in the city, that he would want to entertain him? And he would put Jesus at the head of the table saying: "The Lord is here" yet he would pass by one in need! You don't give money to those you see in need unless you want them to remain there, needing money. Instead give them riches in your imagination! My friend didn't give the man one penny - he inherited his wealth; but he did give his friend the gift of his talent, thereby multiplying it. He is among those called O blessed of my Father, come inherit the Kingdom of God. Why?

Because he gave of the one talent God gave him and fed the hungry, gave drink to the thirsty, and clothed the naked. When his friend was financially in prison and sick at heart because of his limitation, he didn't give him one nickel, but by exercising his God given talent, he multiplied it. This is what I am talking about. Use the talent that God gave you. Don't bury it, afraid to test its power. Exercise each talent, and as you do, your five will make ten. If you can only use two, use them to the best of your ability and they will increase. Then you will be highly commended, for you are not called upon to share physically with others, but to use your imagination and see them as you would like to be seen, were you in their position. If you were in need, would you not appreciate someone imagining you are affluent? That's what my friend did and that's what I am asking you to do.

Take me seriously and use your wonderful talent on the right side. We are told that as a shepherd separates the flock, placing the sheep on the right and the goats on the left, so will our heavenly Father separate us. It is said in a harsh way, that those on the left did not apply their talents and are therefore condemned to everlasting hell; but that simply means that when you seem to die here, you enter the same world and continue until you finally take your talent and use it. Everyone is going to die. That's the greatest certainty in the world. If you tell someone who is about to be married that they will be parted in death, they would think you were horrid, so you don't tell them. But when you die here you are instantly restored to life in a world just like this one, even though you may have given a million dollars to a church or a museum, for that's not using your talent.

When you treat any one as Christ, you do it unto me. And that joy you will feel as you do it! So, I said to my friend, the doctor, regardless of who comes through your door, be it the richest man in town or the poorest, treat Christ and watch what happens in your world. When were you in want? When you saw it in another. And when you saw him thirsty, hungry, and naked and gave him not, that's when you did not do it to me. It's just as simple as that. If you put your hand in your pocket and give him anything, quite often you are simply perpetuating a bum; but when you think of him as well dressed, affluent and healthy in mind and body, that's when you did it unto me. You are only doing it to yourself, really, for Christ is the reality, the true identity of every being. The lady of the evening is Christ making a living. Instead of condemning her, lift her up in your mind's eye and see her affluent. She can still play the same part if she so desires, but take her out of the gutter. And remember: God is doing everything that man is doing, for God is man and there is nothing but God in the world. When you can see this, you will live by it and change your world.

Do what my friend did concerning the barber. He first made sure the man wanted to be a barber, then he gave out of his wonderful human imagination by seeing him successful. Desiring a barber in his neighborhood so that he wouldn't have to start looking for another, he anchored him there. Now the man owns the business and it is the busiest shop in town. And his co-worker now discusses his weekend on the cabin cruiser, his new car, or the party he had in his enlarged home, for these are the things my friend gave him and the man is totally unaware of the giver!

Now let us go into the silence.

By Blood *and* Water

y subject this morning is taken from the First Epistle of John. Now these twenty-one letters (or as we call them, epistles) are not really addressed to individuals or groups. They are mysteries, as is the entire Bible. Whether the Bible in the Old Testament tells the story in the form of history, or whether they tell it in the form of a parable, or whether in the form of a letter, they are all revelations of the mind of God expressed in symbolism. Now, I do not claim that I can give you an exhaustive interpretation of any single story of the Bible. Because they are revelations of the mind of the Infinite, no single interpretation could ever be exhaustive. On one level it may be true, and then you and I expand in consciousness and we re-read the letter and see it differently, and a further expansion in consciousness causes us - even when we re-read it for the fiftieth time - to still see the letter in a different light. So, in this morning's interpretation I will try to keep it on a level that is most practical.

We are told in the First John, 5: "This is He that came by water and blood even Jesus Christ, not by water only, but by water and blood." So, these are symbols of birth. Every natural birth in the world is accompanied by the flowing of water and blood. It's trying to tell the individual of a certain mystery of birth, but he uses the words Christ Jesus and that is the symbol of a truly mysterious birth - something out of nothing. That is the mystery. Out of death, life. Man cannot conceive it. How can something alive come out of that which is dead - how can something come out of nothing? Man accepts it in the mineral world, for he sees, if he goes back far enough in time (he could push the mystery in some remote past), he will accept the fact that sometime, in a way not known to modern science, out of non-organic substance came organism. He will call it by some little tiny name: an amoeba, and that will satisfy his mind. But he stops; he still will not admit that he stated that there was a non-organic substance, or nothing, or something that was dead, out of which came life, out of which came something. He doesn't want to wrestle with that problem, so he leaves that, jumps over the pages of history, and comes to some little thing more complex. Then he teaches evolution from that state. But when he goes far enough back he finds no answer for the appearance of life out of nothing or death.

So here is the mystery. It comes by water and by blood - not by water only, but by water and blood. This is the great mystery of the incarnation, the death, and the resurrection. What incarnation? What death, and what resurrection? The mind instantly thinks in terms of 2,000 years ago and we think that was the great mystery. But before I jump into the mystery let me quote you the very last verse of this wonderful 5th chapter: "Little children keep yourselves from idols." No matter how officialdom justifies them and tells you this is the image of your savior revealed through the minds of a saint or a great artist, you are warned in this chapter to keep yourselves free of idols, in harmony with the second commandment: "Thou shall make no graven image unto the Lord thy God." No matter how it is justified by officialdom or orthodox society, you are asked please not to make anything external to your own mind and bow before it as creative power, for here he is trying to reveal the true creative power that is in man. It sleeps in man as his passive mind. As you unfold the mystery, it awakens from its passive state into its active state, and the birth of active mind is truly the resurrection of Christ in man. It is Christ in man. It is Christ in man that is the hope and the glory.

Now, here in another verse he gives you a test. He asks you to ask whatsoever thing in this world in my name, that the Father may give it you. He did not restrict you to one desire; ask whatsoever thing you desire in my name and the Father will give it to you. Now, if you take it literally, as I have heard thousands of prayers in my own home... Raised in a Christian atmosphere, we said grace at meals and Mother invariably said it, and invariably ended with the words: "For Jesus' sake, amen" - but nothing happened. We ate the food and enjoyed the food. And you will say prayers, long verbal appeals to God for something, always ending: "For Jesus' sake, amen," thinking that if I said it was for his sake that I would thus tempt my Father to give it to me. For did he not say: "Whatsoever thing ye desire, ask it in my name, and the Father will give it to you"? Well, you ask it forever in that name, and nothing happens - therefore, he didn't understand the mystery. So, what is the mystery? Even Jesus Christ, who came not by water only, but by water and the blood.

We have put it into the most practical manner in the world - something out of nothing, life out of death. Conceive of something you desire. Just think of it. The mere thinking of something - that is a conception unaided by another. Is that not an "immaculate conception?" You knew no one in the formulation of your desire. Now you intend to "realize it." It is clear in your mind's eye; it is a holy conception, it is a virgin conception. Can you bring about that something that seemingly is not existing - it is non-existent, it has no existence in fact - and embody it? Can you incarnate it? For this is the mystery of the incarnation that comes by water and blood. Here is a birth that could take place if I am willing to give it human parentage. I must give it human parentage. It cannot of itself be born, for unless I myself become it, it cannot be born; so, I desire to be something other than what I am.

Now what is the water? The water is the great mystery, the great psychological truth that I must discover which will enable me, if I accept it, to live a life according to that truth and give expression to my desire. For water is the truth and the blood is the application of that truth. I could know everything in the world to be known of the mystery, but never live by it - still continue to live as I have always lived, passively accepting the evidence of my senses as fact, accepting the dictates of reason as my guide. I could overhear a conversation or could read it in a book, or hear it in a place like this on Sunday morning. That if you desire something intensely and you truly desire it, and you have a clear mental picture of what you would like to be or what you would like to accomplish, or what you would like another friend to realize - you know exactly what you would like in this world. Now, this is the water by which it could be born. But it cannot be born of water only; it must be born of water and blood. So, I will give you the water. When you know what you want, you make as vivid and as lifelike a representation of what you would see, of what you would hear, and what you would do, were you physically present and physically moving about in such a situation.

To take an example: Suppose I desired a certain apartment, or home, or business. (Take one, so you will not be confused. We will take an apartment.) But reason tells me I cannot afford it. Reason tells me I haven't enough furniture for so big an apartment. Reason tells me a thousand things that would deny that I could ever realize it, but I still would like it. Now this is what I would give you in the form of water, for something must come out of nothing and life out of death. To embody that state, I make it real. You pull it seemingly from a state that is non-existent, therefore something out of nothing. To make it real and to incarnate it and to become alive to it and it to you, you are pulling life out of death.

Now this is what you do. There is a death involved but it is not the kind of death that men call death. There is a death - there is a radical change of state of mind. You completely give up the belief that you are not living in such a place. That is irrational. But that is what you are called upon to do, to completely deny the evidence of your senses and to boldly assume that you are already in that state that you occupy. There you dwell in a state that reason denies. You dwell in an assumption that your senses deny. That is not just the water. If you do it, you are applying the blood. If you are told to do it you are given the truth, for it will work. That water, if you could only add the blood to it, will bring the invisible state into the visible world, and what seemingly is non-existent will crystallize and harden into fact. But if you only know it as too many of us know it, and think the mere knowledge is enough, we will come here on Sunday and thoroughly enjoy this wonderful hour - the music, the message, the meditation, the feeling of companionship you find here. And the whole thing is a thrill for an hour - but such knowledge cannot bring Christ Jesus to birth. In this state, Christ Jesus (now I'll analyze it for you) on a lower plane the word, "Jesus" (Heb. Jeshua) means "salvation, to save."

So, if I desire something and I don't realize it, then I simply continue a life of frustration. If I realize my objective, I have been saved from frustration. Take a simple matter: Suppose I wanted a suit of clothes because I was in need of raiment. If I don't realize the suit of clothes, I am not saved from my nudity. If I realize the suit of clothes, I have been saved. For this is an all- inclusive savior, not just a man. If I wanted water, literal water, a lecture will not quench my thirst. If I wanted food, literal food, the most wonderful revelation would not actually satisfy my hunger. So, Jesus is all-inclusive, meaning everything you desire. He is it, because if you embodied that desire, you embodied your Jesus. Now, to embody Jesus, he cannot be embodied by the knowledge of what to do only. He can only be embodied by the application of that knowledge. So, the knowledge of what to do is called water, the "water of truth"; but the use of that lovingly is called the flowing (shedding) of the blood.

So here we find the symbols that always accompany birth, that which is presented in this mystery. You are told the limit is within you. You make the limit; there is no limit. Whatsoever you desire, ask in my name, for name simply means nature. If I wanted to be in a house and to feel that I am the occupant of that house, there is a certain feeling, a certain nature that goes with it. I must appropriate it as though it were true. Here I am called upon to bring something alive out of a state that is dead. For if I told you what I have done, you would question my sanity and you would feel I am trying to give expression to something that is being pulled out of nothing. For you cannot see it -you don't see me in the house, you don't see me actually occupying and enjoying the life that you know I desire to enjoy. So, if I persist in that assumption, to you (if you should know my persistence) you might think I am headed towards a form of insanity. But if tomorrow the house becomes an embodied fact and I the occupant, then you look at it passively and you will still try to justify it by tracing its appearance back to a visible cause. You will see that in some way, unknown to you, my resources were lifted up, that in some way I became more eligible for that house and you will trace it back to a change in my fortune. You will trace it back to a change in something in my world, but you won't trace these changes back to the unseen assumption in which I dwell.

So, as the mystic tells us in Hebrews 11: "Things unseen were not made of things that do appear." Man refuses to accept it, so he takes everything in his world and tries to take it back to some visible cause, even with the aid of his microscope. He takes the microscope and he will peer through it to prove to his own satisfaction there is a visible, tangible cause; or he goes off into space with his telescope. He must find in the outer world causes of the changes in the outer world. He cannot believe that the whole vast outer world is held together from within. And if we are only on the surface looking at it from without - trying to analyze it and to understand it from without and all that appears without - though it seems there, it isn't. It is all from within, all within the mind of man, and that is the mystery!

So do not make an idol, no matter who makes you the idol, no matter what holy man tells you this is a wonderful thing that will bless you. There is no blessing in states on the outside. Bow to nothing on the outside. We have wondered why throughout the centuries a certain race of people did not become greater sculptors, greater artists in the form of painting, great religious teachers. Maybe they were really taking that second commandment very, very seriously. Make no graven image - no not one- unto me. Make nothing that is graven, that is objective, as image of your Father that is free, for I AM Spirit. If you were to worship me, worship me in spirit and in truth but not in anything that you can turn to on the outside and bend the knee before, whether it be a church, a synagogue, or some statue that hangs upon your wall. He is not there. He is in your mind. He is housed within you; there is the living God within the temple and the temple is man. "Ye are the temple of the living God."

So when I speak of the water and the blood, I speak not of the things that you can see with the eye, such as water and blood. They are only symbolized functions of the mind and the function first comes with water. I must first know what to do before I can do it. So, water comes first. He takes water and puts it into a stone jar gives it something like a shape, and from that stone jar filled with water, he draws - not water, but he converts it; he draws wine (blood).

So here is the first miracle. I know what to do. I take this little world of mine that is one, and then I extract from it something that is not seen. Not quite as hard as that - I call it water. I see something bringing all this into being. I know how it's brought into being. That a man living in luxury is not to be judged harshly because he has it and you haven't it. He is living in a state of consciousness that solidifies in the form that you see now and call luxurious. One in a state of health, one who is recognized, one who is accomplished, one who is contributing much to the world -don't judge them. These are states made visible. Find out if you can. Get into a similar state. He is not occupying the only state in the world. There are infinite states and if you try even to duplicate that state (if it can be duplicated, or you can get close to it or you can transcend it) find out within your own mind's eye what you want. Don't be envious of him. Leave him alone for he is applying the law. He is entitled to everything in this world that he can actually conceive and desire and put himself into and live it, for man is living in an infinite world of invisible states and an individual wisely or foolishly occupies a state. While he remains faithful to the state, the state will externalize and become the circumstances and the conditions of his life. The moment he detaches himself in consciousness from that state, the things that he enjoyed before vanish from his world.

Now, if everything in my world depends upon a state of consciousness, it would be the height of insanity to seek the thing before I actually fix within myself the state on which the thing depends, for that which requires a state of consciousness to produce its effect cannot be effected without such a state of consciousness. So, when I know what I want, to support that there is an invisible state of consciousness. The world calls that invisible state a non-existing nothingness. They cannot even call it a thing, for to them it has no existence, no reality. That is the mystery: a self-begotten child conceived unaided by another and carried faithfully in the womb of God - which is the mind of man. It was placed there without the aid of another, by man's desire. That was the immaculate conception; that's the virgin conception.

Now, the virgin birth - can I bring it from its invisible state and really make it a tangible fact within my world? Try it! As you try it with one thing and you succeed, you will try it with two and four and eight and so on, and eventually the sleeping giant in man - which is the Son of God in man called Christ - will awaken. He will awaken by moving from the passive state to the active state. The passive state is simply the complete and utter surrender of man to appearances, to live believing that life is on the outside, and he moves from that state where he surrenders and believes all these things to be causes to the active state, where he puts everything in subjection to that something within himself which is his awakened imagination. He imagines a thing to be so; he persuades himself that it is so and walks faithful to his assumption.

Then you will know why in Romans 14 he tells us that every man be fully persuaded in his own mind (don't persuade her, leave her alone). You persuade yourself of the changes you desire expressed in her. If you desire a change in your relationships at home or in business, you don't argue, you don't persuade them. Let every man be fully persuaded in his own mind. So, can I persuade myself that you are as I desire to see you? Then, to the degree that I can persuade myself, you will conform in the outer world to that persuasion. If I hope to see changes there before I myself will start the change on the inside, the chances are I will hope in vain. You, yourself, may desire certain changes and I might see them change in my world, but they were not caused because I moved into an active state. I am still reflective, and most of us in this world are reflecting life; and the purpose of a church of this nature is to make us not reflect but to affect life. If I affect, then Christ is awakened within me. If I only reflect it, then I sleep with Adam, and the purpose is to move from the sleep of Adam to the wakefulness of the Son of God called Christ. Adam too, is called the son of God but in the state of profound sleep. But he moves from that state of sleep - or the passive state of mind - to the active state, will be no nearer the proving of it than you are now. But if you took a little bit, one drop of this water, and went out even to disprove it - in order to disprove it, you must seriously and sincerely try it. If you try it, you won't disprove it. You will be encouraged to drink more water and still more and bring about this birth of your savior, and you decide what will save you today from your present predicament. It may be a job, it may be an increase of funds, it may be companionship, it may be something I don't know - but whatever it is that you this day desire (and unless you get it you feel thwarted, you feel frustrated), then it would save you if you got it. Now take that as your savior. Look into your mind's eye and see it clearly. It may seem almost sacrilegious to the orthodox mind to tell you that when you see clearly in your mind's eye the state desired - either for self or another - you are actually looking into the face of Jesus, for you are seeing the state that could save you from where you are or what you are.

So, you try it and the mind will expand. You will find yourself not only increasing in this world, in the outer world, but you will find mystical revelations taking place within you, which is the purpose of the teaching. It is not just to bring about changes in the inner that man ascends on higher levels of consciousness. The purpose of the whole appearance is to awaken from the lowest descent on the ladder to the highest. He is ascending to the highest, for we are told in the vision of Jacob: above it all stood God - on the ladder stood these heavenly beings ascending and descending - but above all stood God. So, the real destiny of man is to reach the height that he may awaken as God.

So, the mystery is: God became man that man may become God. He came down as man. Take the same verse and give it a higher interpretation. So here God died - yes, died - to become man. The death of God is complete forgetfulness of the fact that he is God. He had to completely forget that he is God, therefore died to awaken as man. If he remembered he was God, he just couldn't be as man, but a complete and utter death, which is forgetfulness that I am God to become man. So, the poet wrote it beautifully and said: "God became man that man may become God." He said: "Unless I die you could not live, but if I die I shall arise again and you with me." Then he goes on to ask a man: "Could you love one who had never died for thee or could you die for one who had not died for thee," and so he is putting this into the most wonderful poetical mystery in the book, "Jerusalem" by Blake.

He reveals to the mind who can see it, that you who believe yourself because you are visible, and you must do what man passively must do - he traces your origin back to a germ. As long as you began as a germ, you are no more than a big germ. If you begin as something else, you are only something enlarged of the same thing. For all ends run true to origins. If I can take you back where you cannot see it, and take you back to the great mystery that you are actually begotten of God - if your origin is God, your end is God. If your origin is a bug then your end is a bug. So you have the "choice." The passive mind (which is really the scientific mind) must still insist on finding causes external to itself. It cannot find causes in that passive state within itself.

I tell you: the great mystery is that you came out of a seeming death. It is a death. God died to become man, because he desired the companionship of men as Gods, as the poet told us:

Man should not stay a man.
His aim should higher be.
For God will only Gods accept as company.

So you cannot in your present state of the passive mind be companions of your Father, who longs and desires that every son, every child, awakens to become companions of Deity. So, to do it, he had to die as God, and became his creation in the hope that the creation would awaken and become his companion.

But you see he gave us such a gift. He completely freed me of the responsibility of returning. I don't have to awaken; I am as free as the wind. He gave me complete freedom of will. I may hurt myself, ruin myself, but because of the gift of God to me, to make me alive, he cannot interfere and make me awake. He may appeal through awakened children and they may appeal to their sleeping brother, but they cannot by the same law interfere and make me awake. They can only appeal and try in some subtle way to suggest, but the gift was absolute. God gave himself to become me, finding myself, man. I think my origin was man, so my destiny - no matter how big a man I become, no matter how wise a man - it will still be a man. But if my origin is God my destiny is God, and I will awaken one day to discover this wonderful unfolding mystery within me.

Now let us go into the silence.

Christ Bears Our Sins

eter tells us that Christ bears our sins in his body on the cross. And the prophet Isaiah said: "He takes our infirmities and bears our diseases."

Who is this being who bears our sins, our infirmities, and our diseases? Christ! Our wonderful human imagination! When you are in pain, or experiencing deep sorrow, your imagination is doing the suffering. If a friend tells you he is not feeling well, or is in great pain, and you tell him that his imagination - called Christ - is doing the suffering, your friend would not believe you, because he conceives Christ to be someone other than himself. But Christ is the human imagination, and until man discovers this for himself the Bible will make no sense to him whatsoever.

We are told: "In the beginning was the Word, and the Word was with God and the Word was God. The Word became flesh and dwells in us." That word is your I Am! And if the Word is God and dwells in you as your awareness, is not God doing the suffering when you say, I am suffering? Having just revealed God's name, you are confessing that God is in pain; therefore, does He not bear all the sufferings of the world in his body while he is on the cross of mankind?

When I speak of the joy of awakening to the knowledge of who God really is, I would think everyone would be eager to experience that awareness; yet only an nth part will say, Yes! A friend wrote, saying: "My husband applied for and received a temporary position as a carpenter, working for the Los Angeles school system. When he was let out he said, `They will call me back for another temporary period.' I suggested that if he wanted to work there on a permanent basis he could, if he would imagine it. Instead he gave me all kinds of reasons why a permanent position was not possible.

"Recently he was called back for another temporary position. When I reminded him of what he had imagined six months ago he did not want to recognize his harvest of the seed he had planted and became very angry. As he spoke, our souls made contact and I heard him say, `I am asleep and don't you dare awaken me!' "

Her husband, like 99% of the people of the world, does not want to be awakened, feeling that if he awakens to a higher level he will lose the pleasures of the flesh.

A friend, a very successful playwright, with many famous stars as his clients, used to listen to my visions and my interpretations of scripture for a short time, then tell me he had heard enough. He didn't want to go beyond the point of curiosity, to become interested and desire the spiritual world, because he was afraid he would lose his physical contact with life and he was only interested in sex. He had money and everything money could buy, and he loved playing the field in the theatrical world.

He died a few years ago and is now restored to a body just like the one he had here, only young, full of vigor, eager to continue his sexual life. This man has not felt the famine which is sent. It is not a hunger for food or a thirst for water, but for the hearing of the word of God. And until that famine possesses you God's word will not hold your interest. I could go on the radio and TV or write articles for the newspapers regarding my experiences, but - like the lady's husband - they would say, "I am asleep and don't you dare awaken me!"

Now, God and his word are one, so if God sent his word, then he sent himself declaring: "He who sees me, sees him who sent me; for I am the word which will not return unto me void, but must accomplish that which I purpose and prosper in the thing for which I was sent."

The outer man is the external word, which comes first. The inner man is then sent to animate and eventually give life to the outer man by fulfilling the word. And when the outer man hungers for the word of God, everything said in scripture concerning God's plan of self-redemption fulfills itself in him. He doesn't redeem someone else, as there is no one else. We are the gods who came down and God can only redeem himself by fulfilling scripture.

Now another lady shared this vision saying: "I am standing in the midst of an enormous crowd. Everyone around me is screaming, `He is crazy. He is mad. He is crazy. He is mad,' over and over again. Walking quickly to discover who they are referring to, I see a man standing alone at the head of the crowd. Recognizing him as the man I love, I run to him and cry, `I love you, I love you.'

"Although the crowd surges upon him and beats him, I continue to express my love. Suddenly he places his hands upon my neck. I feel his thumbs press into my throat and feel as though I am going to die. Then the pressure is released. The man raises his hands, which become two white wings, which caress me with an indescribable love as I awake."

That night this lady fulfilled the 40th, 48th, 51st, 52nd and 53rd chapters of Isaiah. I say to her without any doubt in my heart, that she is very near salvation. Everything in her wonderful vision was made visible. She was the man and the crowd. She sent herself through hell because she loves herself, just as you and I do. In Blake's lovely song,

> *"A Little Boy Lost", he said:*
> *"Nought loves another as itself,*
> *Nor venerates another so.*
> *Nor is it possible to thought*
> *A Greater than itself to know."*

How can thought know a thought greater than itself? How could you love another more than yourself? It is impossible, for there is no other.

Love is the being playing every part. Love is the crowd, the tempters, and the one abused. Feel distress, and you are abusing Christ by saying, I am distressed. Feel ashamed, limited, inadequate or afraid, and God is experiencing them all; for He is your awareness, believing himself to be ashamed, limited, inadequate, or afraid and dying in your sins.

Just as my friend heard the vision tell her to change the comma, for the statement should read: "Before Abraham, was I am," here again we find that unless you believe your I am is the one you have worshiped on the outside, you die in your sins; for your I am was before Abraham.

It is Christ who bears all of your afflictions, your sorrows and diseases. There is no record of a man who took upon himself a terminal disease while the one he took it from was set free. The implication is there, for - bearing our afflictions and weakness - God has the power to set man free. But Christ is not someone external to yourself. The Universal Christ is a diffusion of an individuality. You say I am, I say I am. We are the same I am, who is Christ, who is God, who is Jehovah - for there is nothing but I am!

Christ, who is your very self, bears all of your afflictions, your weaknesses, and sins; but this is difficult for man to understand. Several years ago I gave a series of nineteen lectures in San Francisco, attended by a lady and her lawyer son. At the end of the series the lady questioned her son, saying: "Do you believe Neville?" And answering with his rational mind he said: "He sounds sincere. He may be sincerely wrong, but I'm sure he is sincere."

At that time the son was living with his mother. Every night before retiring they would remind each other to put the law of identical harvest into practice. When I returned to San Francisco the next year I learned that this man had formed an organization which was in the process of building the largest and most modern co-op in the Bay Area, called the Comstock. This project was followed by building up the peninsula and now this gentleman is worth millions.

Both mother and son used the law to achieve their every goal, yet she admitted she did not understand what I meant when I said Christ suffers for her. Although she could tell me: "I have a toothache," she couldn't grasp the fact that she is her imagination and therefore the cause of the toothache as well as the wonderful co-op.

If you are suffering, Christ is suffering, for his name is I am, and there is no other Christ. God actually became flesh and dwells in you.

Once you realize this you will never turn to another. This gentleman has made a fortune, yet he does not understand how it all came about, because the hunger is not upon him. Although it would not be necessary, he is not willing to give up his enormous earthly holdings to have the experiences which would result in regeneration.

You do not kill desire. You do not have yourself castrated. You are simply beyond the organization of sex and your desire for earthly things ceases to be. Ninety-nine per cent of the people here desire worldly pleasures, while I speak of a pleasure that transcends this world - where one lives in a world of reality and creativity. But until that famine comes, you will continue to desire things that die in this world.

Now, another lady shared this experience, saying: "In my vision I knew you had died, yet you had returned to lecture and teach as usual. You were wearing my earthly father's face, yet I knew the bone structure to be yours. Everyone called you the Father, but not knowing my earthly father, they could not see his face, only yours. As I woke I knew that the face I touched on the surface would be that of my earthly father, but its structure would be that of the Father."

There is only one Father. It is He who wears every mask. In this wonderful experience, she saw her earthly father wearing the frame of the Father, because the Father is a protean being and assumes every face. She saw the foundation, the bone structure of the man who told her salvation's story, wearing the face of her earthly father.

We are told that when God took upon himself the sins of the world, he was a man of sorrow, despised and rejected by men. There is no description of the man in whom God awoke because he is never a sculptured, beautiful man on the outside, but a perfectly normal person.

This lady said that she is very fond of the Book of John, as it seems to be more loving than any other book in the Bible. I will go along with that. She felt that the answer to the experience I just spoke of would come to her from the Book of John. I suggest she read the 10th chapter of John. In it Christ is called a man who has a devil and they question why listen to him. You, my dear, are that central figure, and you are also the crowd screaming at yourself; and you deny the existence of the Christ within, for there is no other. There is only God.

You can put God to the test, and if He proves himself in the testing then you will know God is your own wonderful human imagination. If you want the joy of marriage, a love affair, or a romance, you can test God by assuming the one you desire is with you now. And to the degree you persist in that assumption, it will be yours to experience. Do not be concerned as to how or when it will happen; simply persist in the assumption that it has happened, and when it does you will know who God is.

My wife woke too early to get up this morning, so she thought about what she wanted most, and that was for her husband and daughter to be blissfully happy. Thinking of what she could do to make it so, she realized that it was something they alone must decide. Then she fell asleep dwelling on their happiness and this is her dream: Seeing me lying on a couch she heard me say: "I don't feel comfortable here," and she replied: "I know - you don't like to sleep on the first floor, but would rather be elevated and sleep above."

Then the dream changed and she was putting a puzzle together with our daughter Vicki, who began to laugh as she picked up a piece of the puzzle and watched it fall into its perfect place. Looking at Vicki she said to herself: "I have never seen her look so pretty and be so blissfully happy." Then she awoke. Her desire for happiness was answered in the depth of her being and must now come to the surface.

Jesus Christ is your own wonderful human imagination and his story is all about you. Told in the third person, it is written as though another is doing all the suffering for you; yet you know you are the one who is suffering. I tell you, that unless you believe your awareness of being is God you will continue to miss your mark, thereby remaining in sin.

I am is the key to scripture. Called Jesus Christ in the New Testament, God the Father's name is revealed in the Old Testament as I am. Having come into the world to fulfill the word, you cannot return empty but must accomplish that which you purposed and prosper in the thing for which you sent yourself. After inspiring the prophets to tell your story, you came not only to fulfill their prophecy, but to share your experiences to encourage others.

The Old Testament is a prophetic blueprint which you will fulfill, for you are the Jehovah of the Old Testament and the Jesus Christ of the New. You may either accept this truth or reject it, but what I am telling you is true. Christ is not a little man, but the universally diffused individuality of which we are. So, when one awakes and the second one follows, the third will awaken and eventually all of the universally diffused individuals will awaken in that one glorious body called the kingdom of heaven. Having come into and overcoming the world of death, we will be victorious over our challenge.

The men of science tell us that the universe is melting and will one day come to its end. I am not going to question this, but I do know that Imagination came into this world of death to overcome it. I also know that nothing dies, because we are the immortal Imagination who clothed himself in these garments of flesh which die, but we - their life-giving spirit - cannot die.

I cannot force anyone to want my experiences. My family in Barbados all live in comfort and know they earn much more than I do. They judge a man by what he has in this world and are not interested in who he is. They cannot understand why a man of my age continues to do what I am doing, when I could move to Barbados and live in clover with all expenses paid by the business. And I can't persuade them to listen to me because the hunger is not upon them.

Until that hunger for the hearing of the word of God possesses you, you will continue to be possessed by the world. You may become the Pope, but that does not mean you hunger for the word of God. It may mean that you hunger for the power that rests in the office of the Pope, the hunger to be recognized and praised. But when the hunger to experience the word of God possesses you, you will know you - the Word - sent yourself. You will then understand the words: "He who sees me, sees him who sent me," for you will fulfill God's word.

There must be two witnesses: one external and one internal. The external witness is scripture, and you who have the spiritual experience are the internal witness. Knowing your experiences parallel the scriptures, you know that the Father in the depths of your own being watches to see that all the pieces are in place and the image of his declared purpose is perfect.

Having prophesied what must take place, God will fulfill it; and you - the image of the invisible God - will radiate his glory and become the express image of his person. Then you will be used as the bone structure on which every face will be placed to reveal to the one who has the experience, the meaning of being God the Father.

In my friend's vision everyone referred to me as the Father. Her father was a father, but I am the Father upon which every father's face is placed. She was aware that I had died and had returned, only to tell the story of God's plan of salvation in order to redeem myself, for there is only God in the world.

Now let us go into the silence.

Christh In You

"Examine yourselves to see if you are holding to your faith. Test yourselves! Do you not realize that Jesus Christ is in you?" Now, faith is not complete until through experiment it becomes experience! When you test the Christ in you and prove from experience that it works, then you have the faith. But first you must find who Christ is, where he is, and what he is. You are not called upon to test a tradition of man as something on the outside, but Jesus Christ who is in you!

Perhaps you heard on the news tonight that the Catholics have just eliminated forty saints. For hundreds of years millions of people have prayed to Saint Christopher, yet now they are being told that he never existed. How many St. Christopher medals and figurines were sold to protect those who went into battle or traveled afar? Believing he was the saint of the traveler, how many put their faith in him? Santa Barbara was named after Saint Barb, who is now believed to be non-existent, yet the cause of the recent broken oil line!

If you will read scripture carefully (and not go along with the herd) you will see that there is no intermediary between yourself and God. No priest or saint, minister, truth teacher, or so-called healer can be an intermediary between you and God. Christ in you is your hope of glory. You must examine yourself to see if you are holding to this faith. Test yourself. Do you not realize that Jesus Christ is in you? If you do, put him to the test. He is your power to create, your power to imagine everything - be it good, bad, or indifferent.

The 14th chapter of the Book of John begins: "Let not your hearts be troubled." This statement is repeated in different ways over and over again by the master of souls - who is Christ in you, for when he awakens fear is abolished. Awake, he urges you to fear not, be not afraid, be not troubled. A tyrant could not exist without fear. He must scare us to death before he can rule us. By slaughtering millions (and you are afraid you will be next) he has you under his power. But if you know you and your family cannot die, you will not be afraid and there would be no tyrant. Tyranny can exist only in a frightened world. So, Awakened Imagination begins the 14th chapter of John by saying: "Let not your heart be troubled, you believe in God, believe also in me. In my Father's house are many mansions. If it were not so would I have told you that I go to prepare a place for you? And when I go and prepare a place for you, I will come again and take you to myself, that where I am there you may be also. Now the place you know and the way you know." Then Thomas said, 'Lord, we do not know where you are going, so how can we know the way?' and he replied, 'I am the way and the truth and the life.' Then Philip said, 'Show us the Father and we will be satisfied.' And he answered, 'I have been so long with you and yet you do not know me Philip? He who has seen me has seen the Father. How then can you say, 'Show us the Father?'"

Let us take this verse on this level first and then take it into the higher level. In my Father's house are many mansions. The word translated "mansion" means to stay in a certain place; state; relation; or expectancy." There are infinite states from which you may view the world. You may enter a state and abide there until it becomes your home or you could be simply passing through for a moment, but it is a state, one of your Father's mansions. Choose the mansion in your Father's house that you would like to enter. Assume you are already there. Feel the reality of the state surround you and you have arrived. Your dream is now true, but you must abide there!

When you leave this auditorium tonight you expect to return to the place you left to come here. At the moment this auditorium is solid and real, while your home is only a mental image. So, what is a home? It is the state to which your thoughts most constantly return. Are you thinking from the state you desire? Or is your dream just a passing fancy, a daydream you enjoyed for the moment and then dropped? You can tell if you abide in your house of desire by watching your thoughts, for the state in which you most constantly return constitutes your dwelling place.

When you imagined you were the person you wanted to be and heard your friends rejoice at your good fortune, you entered that state and prepared a place in which to dwell; for at that moment Christ in you was speaking to the outer, rational you. As your own wonderful human imagination Christ is telling you that he knows you are afraid, that you have obligations in life which must be met, but to not be afraid for "I will go and prepare a place for you." Knowing this, close your physical eyes upon the world round about you and let not your heart be troubled, neither let it be afraid, for all things are possible to Christ in you! Let him prepare the state, for he is the way to its fulfillment.

Closing your eyes against the facts of life, dare to assume you are seeing and hearing what you would see and hear if your desire were true. Now, tune it in as you would a radio. If, when you turned on the radio four or five stations are heard at the same time, you couldn't stand the confusion and would turn the radio off. So, it is with your imagination - it must be fine-tuned. Now no radio or TV is comparable to you, for that which the mind creates cannot be greater than the mind who created it. We are amazed at the perfection of a little instrument called a radio because it can produce sound out of the nowhere, yet the mind that is so amazed is the one who created it. Our radio or television can be carried around the house or yard with no connection to a charge of electricity, yet the sound and picture come through perfect, and any station (or channel) can be reached by merely a flick of the wrist. At this moment everything that is being broadcast or telecast in the world is in this room, but we haven't tuned it in.

Now, you have an instrument infinitely greater than any radio or television, but it must be turned on and fine-tuned. Think of a friend who would truly rejoice in your good fortune. Tune him in until his is the only voice you can hear. Let him tell you of his thrill because of your good fortune. Listen carefully until his voice is crystal clear and you can hear the sentence you put upon that voice. Now, believe in its reality. If you will, you are living by this principle and not merely accepting the Christian faith as a substitute for living by it.

Can you imagine the turmoil which is going on in the Catholic world tonight now that the courts have cut off forty of their so-called saints? Half of my family is Catholic. I do hope that my Protestant brothers, who did not marry Catholic girls, will be big enough to mention it. I recall about twenty years ago my wife and I visited a Catholic family. At the time my wife said to me: "They are ardent Catholics, but don't know a thing about you except that you are a Protestant and not saved." After a lovely dinner we sat around the pool and watched their three sons swim. Each boy wore a St. Christopher's medal around his neck. One was three years into the priesthood when he quit, joined the army, and returned minus his hearing. Another returned without a foot and the third minus an arm. They told me that they believed that without this medal they would have died. Well, I wonder what will happen to that family when they learn St. Christopher never existed! The only Christ who ever existed is within you as your own wonderful human imagination. There never was another.

When one being awoke to discover all that was foretold in scripture was taking place in him, he knew who the Messiah really was. He told his story, while some believed and some did not believe him. Those who heard and believed him wrote his experiences in the form of a story, because truth is far more acceptable when told in story form, as in our four gospels. But one day we will be big enough to hear it without the story form to support us.

Redemption was foretold in the Old Testament, but not understood by those who recorded it. The prophets who prophesied the coming of the Messiah searched and inquired concerning this grace that was to be ours, and it was revealed to them that it was not for them to know. The time had not yet come, for it was for us. Now that the horrors have been fulfilled, the Messiah who was buried in us before that the world was is beginning to erupt in the individual.

Everything said of Jesus Christ will be realized in you individually, for the Bible was written about you.

Now, before the Messiah comes, you can put his word to the test. If Christ is your own wonderful human imagination and all things - be they good, bad, or indifferent - are made by him, you can imagine unlovely things and perpetuate their image. To say that Christ makes only the good and a devil makes the evil is false, for the devil is just as phony as Christopher. When you doubt the power of Christ in you - that's the devil. Unless you actually believe that "I am" is the being you are seeking and pray only to him by exercising your human imagination, you will never reach your desire, for awareness is the only power that can give it to you.

Tonight, ask yourself what you would be aware of hearing, seeing and experiencing if your desire were now fulfilled. If what I tell you is true and your imagination is the creator of all things, then you should be able to prove his power in the testing. I tell you: there is no intermediary between yourself and God. If you will but test this power within you, it will prove itself in performance. Then you will know who Christ really is.

Now, no one comes unto the Father except by me and I am going to tell you exactly how to come to the Father. It is not spelled out in scripture. I searched, but could not find him until he revealed himself to me. One day he will reveal himself in you, for you will see a lad, chosen by God to be his son. The lad will be ruddy in complexion, very handsome, with beautiful eyes. He will be in his early teens. As you look into his eyes you know exactly who he is and who you are. Then and only then do you know you are God the Father. So, no one comes to the awareness of being God the Father except by the revelation of David, for he is the one through whom you come to the awareness of Fatherhood.

In this same 14th chapter of John, Awakened Imagination asks this question: "I have been so long with you and yet you do not know me? He who has seen me has seen the Father, how then can you say, 'Show us the Father?'" David is one with his father. He is united to the Lord, having become one spirit with him. So, the only way you can ever find the Father within you is to bring forth his son, David. We are told in the 89th Psalm: "I have found David. He has cried unto me 'Thou art my Father, my God and the Rock of my salvation.'"

The word "found" recorded here, if taken on the surface implies David was lost; but the word means, "to bring forth one who is behind you." David, eternal youth, was put into the mind of man, yet so that man cannot find out what God has done from the beginning to the end when he brings forth that which was behind all along, waiting to come out. You will never know you are God the Father until David appears and calls you Father. It is he who stated in the 2nd Psalm: "I will tell of the decree of the Lord, he said unto me, 'Thou art my son, today I have begotten thee.'" In my own case I felt an explosion in my skull, and when everything settled I saw my son leaning against the side of an open door, looking out on a pastoral scene. As he turned and looked at me standing at his right, I knew I was his father, fulfilling scripture.

The gospel is the truest story ever told but men, because of their traditions, have voided the world of God and built a stupid concept called "saints." What man on earth could be a saint? The only saints are the redeemed, those who form the body of the Risen Lord. May I tell you: everyone is predestined for that redemption. Not one will be lost, so why pick someone out and call him a saint only to later deny he was ever a Christian? They even took Saint Nicolas off their list, claiming he never existed! Here are mortal men, without vision, appointing themselves judges of saints!

I tell you: regardless of what you do here as a mortal man you are redeemed, for redemption hasn't a thing to do with the man's ethical code. It's entirely up to the being within a man who - having played all the parts - awakens to receive the crown of righteousness which has been waiting for your return. The moment he awakens you are redeemed. But your friends know you as mortal and have not the slightest concept of what this power is. Browning said in his "Reverie":

> *"From the first, Power was - I knew*
> *That, strive but for a closer view,*
> *Love were as plain to see.*

This is true for: prior to power, was love. In my own case striving for love did not reveal it to me. Only when God in me unveiled himself as love was it plain to see.

As love, you will exercise your almighty power in the world to come. To have that power here, before you were incorporated into the body of love, would cause havoc in the world; for the God of whom I speak is infinite love and almighty power, and that God you are, but you will not know it until your journey is complete. Only when he completes the journey will he unveil himself to you - his emanation - by embracing you into his own being. At that moment you will cease to be another, for you will become one with the Living God. Then you will tell your story to all who will listen. Some will believe you and others will disbelieve, but you will tell it until you take off your mortal garment for the last time to become one with the Risen Lord who is made up of all the redeemed of humanity. And in the end, when all are redeemed, this being who was before that the world was will be more powerful, more wise, and more glorious, because of his journey into the world of death.

Tonight, learn to fine-tune your imagination. Knowing the voice of your friend, tune him in. Determine the words you want him to say and listen carefully. Tune him in until his words are fine and clear, then believe you heard him. Think it really happened. If you will, it will come to pass. When, I cannot say, for every imaginal act is like an egg and no two eggs (unless they are of the same species) have the same interval of time for hatching. The little bird comes out in three weeks, a sheep in five months, a horse in twelve months, and a human in nine months. Your imaginal act has its own appointed hour to ripen and flower. If it seems long, wait - for it is sure and will not be late for itself.

An imaginal act is a creative act, for the moment it is felt, the seed (or state) is fertilized. It will take a certain length of time to be born, so start today by assuming you are the man (or woman) you would like to be and let the people in your mind's eye reflect the truth of your assumption. Be faithful to your assumption. Persist in this thought, for persistence is the way to bring your desire to pass. You don't persist through effort or fear, rather knowing that your imaginal act is now a fact; wait for its birth, for it will come.

Now, a friend wrote, saying that in her dream she was walking down the street holding a fish in her hands. The fish appeared to be dead, yet she could feel it pulse. Determine to keep the fish alive, she found a cup, filled it with water, and placed the fish inside. Then she awoke, hearing a male voice say: "Oh my darling."

Every dream contains within itself the capacity for symbolic significance. A fish is the symbol of the power of the human imagination. Imagine yourself depressed, and imagination will throw you into the pit of depression. Imagine yourself free, and your imaginative power will bring you out, for your imagination is the savior of your world. When you become lost in the reasoning world, your imagination is not fed with your desire, for reason negates its flow. Christ, being your human imagination, is not limited by the reasoning world and all things are possible to him. If you would ignore the facts and walk in your imaginal acts as though your wish were already fulfilled you are feeding Christ, and he becomes alive within you once more. Her dream, created by her own being who is Christ in her, was telling her she is neglecting herself. Knowing what to do is not enough. Knowledge must be acted upon. It is so easy to accept the Christian faith and use it only as a substitute for action, and so difficult to live by it; but only as you live by your imagination can you ever know who you really are.

I had a similar experience as this lady's, but mine was in another form of the symbol of Christ, which is the pig. One night I found myself in a nursery filled with everything that grows. As I started to leave I looked down to find a little runt of a pig at my feet. Picking him up, I placed him on a table, broke off some branches of a nearby tree to cushion him, and began to search for food to feed him. Then, as happens in dreams, the scene shifted. I am now in a vegetable market with the pig at my side. He has grown in stature but is very thin. Suddenly I realized that he was mine, so I turned to my little daughter Vicki and said: "Go get me some food that I may feed my pig." She replied: "Daddy, I don't have any money." Then I said: "You don't need money here, for all of this belongs to us." Going over to a stand of crackers, piled in the form of a pyramid, Vicki took a box from the base, causing the entire pyramid to come tumbling down.

Opening the box, I began to feed my pig when my brother Victor came by and, taking what appeared to be white, creamy grease, he spread it on my crackers saying: "This will give it sustenance." Suddenly a lit candle appeared within the mixture and I said: "The candle is lit and it must never go out again." Then these words from scripture came to me: "His candle is lit upon my forehead and by this light I walk through darkness, for the spirit of man is the candle of the Lord."

Prior to this vision I had discovered that my imagination was the only God who ever existed, yet in spite of this discovery I had not fed it. Rather I continued to use the rational approach to life by planning my life on a reasonable basis. Knowing of a power that did not need reason was not enough; I had to exercise this power within me. And then I was determined to exercise my imagination on behalf of myself and others. I saw my candle was lit and knew that from then on I would not let its light go out or get dim for lack of use.

Paul said: "I am a steward of the mystery." The word "steward" means "the keeper of the pig." We are told to follow the example of the dishonest steward and falsify our records. To be a steward of the mysteries, however, the pig must be fed so that you know what you are talking about. You must exercise your powerful imagination morning, noon, and night and never neglect it.

If tonight you gave a man a million dollars to invest well, he will neglect to feed his pig because to him he has it all. Then one night he will see his pig and realize what he has done to the power within him. If you are a musician and stop practicing for a week you will not be qualified to give a concert. Only when you practice daily are you qualified. And so it is with your imagination. It must be exercised daily and then one day you will discover the Christ within you, who is God the Father, who comes only through his son David calling you Father.

Now let us go into the silence.

Christa Is Your Life

his teaching is essentially a revelation of the Risen Christ. I am not speaking of the life of any man between his physical birth and death, but of the Christ who has risen in me and who rises in all. I have no mental image of a being outside of my life, or yours.

Paul tells us: "You have died, and your life is hidden with Christ in God. When Christ who is our life appears, you will appear with him in glory."[2] Here we see Paul equating your life with Christ. You are alive now, so what does Paul mean when he claims you have died? All of Paul's letters equate death with a sleep so profound the past is forgotten. It is from the sleep of death he urges you to roust yourself from saying: "Awake O sleeper and rise from the dead."

The one and only Christ is your life. Now asleep in humanity, this power believes itself to be you. And when it awakens and rises in you, it is you who rise as Christ. God's power and wisdom is sleeping in you as your own life. God is love! When God died he gave you, his sons, your inheritance. It was not a home or some fabulous land, but the power of his love! The power to create every desire of your heart.

Let me start with a point, which has confused some. A gentleman wrote: "You say others have bodies and lives of their own, but their reality is rooted in you as your reality is rooted in God. I have a desire that involves others, yet I have the feeling that they do not want to be a part of it. Although you say I should not concern myself with influencing others, as the world - rooted in me - will play the part they must play if I am faithful to my objectives; but what right have I to influence others?

"Believing that imagining creates reality and that there is no fiction, I start with a premise that has not one thing in the outer world to support it; but in the midst of my project I turn aside, for I

---

[2] Col. 3:3,4

cannot influence these men. I now wonder if perhaps this is also their hidden desire and they do not want me in it. You say when I am lovingly exercising my imagination on behalf of another, I am mediating God to that other. I know that what I imagine will benefit all; yet because of my doubt as to their desire to be involved, should I continue to do it?"

I would say to him, just take the objective. Perhaps because of their talents you have singled them out as partners, but if they moved away would you still have the desire? If so, then they are not essential. If you put yourself in the end by rejoicing in the objective's fulfillment, those who are equally talented - and maybe more so - will come seeking you; for remaining in the end, you will draw the necessary individuals to play the part they must play to aid the birth of what you are doing.

Now, you questioned if all things worked for good. The 8th chapter of Romans tells us that it does. This truth is dramatized for us in the 50th chapter of the Book of Genesis. It is the story of Joseph, one of the twelve Sons of Jacob. Joseph had the capacity to dream vividly. His visions were true and he could interpret them. His brothers, becoming envious, plotted to kill him; but Judah interceded, urging them to sell him instead.

Joseph was sold as a slave, and when no one could interpret Pharaoh's dreams Joseph was brought before him. He interpreted the dreams so accurately, Pharaoh made him equal with himself, and whatever Joseph said was instantly executed. He foretold of the famine that was to come; and when his brothers came seeking food Joseph - now sitting on the throne - recognized them, and said: "Fear not, you meant evil against me, but God meant it for good." So, everything works for good when there is time to reflect upon the act.

I could go back to my own small family. There came a moment in our life when it seemed as though the world had come to its end. My father's partners, desiring to take control of the little equity he had in the business, succeeded and our world collapsed. We had nothing and even our friends made themselves scarce.

But what appeared to be an evil thing turned out to be a blessing, for by detaching ourselves from this partnership - which was small in the sense that they couldn't think big - my father started on his own with sons who could imagine. The family has now turned our business into a large enterprise of many kinds of businesses with no outside partnerships, dwarfing anything we thought possible forty years ago when it happened. It has taken time and reflection, but now we can see that - although my father's partners intended evil against him - God meant it for good.

Now, a friend had a dream in which he received a letter with his son's report card inside, indicating that he must show a decided improvement in four subjects, one of which was algebra. Since his son has always been tops in math, he was annoyed and instantly revised the report card. Suddenly angry with himself he said: "I am tired of the responsibility of this power and life's many needs of revision. My son is a big boy now, let him do it for himself," and awoke.

Peter asked the question: "Lord, if my brother sins against me, how often must I forgive him, seven times?" and the Lord answered: "I did not say seven, but seventy times seven." This does not mean four hundred and ninety times. Seventy is the numerical value of the Hebrew letter *ayin*, whose symbol is an eye. Seven is the numerical value of the Hebrew letter zayin, whose symbol is a sword.

Here we are being told to imagine until the eye is fixed as though nailed with a sword. It may happen the first time or it may take a thousand times to persuade yourself that things are as you desire them to be, and not as they appear to be. But, to the degree that you are self-persuaded that you have done it in your imagination, will the outer world reflect its harmony.

William James, a professor of psychology at Harvard, is one of our great educators. He said: "The greatest revelation in my generation is the discovery that human beings, by a change of inner attitude can produce outer changes in harmony with their inner convictions."

That's in the Bible. In the Book of Genesis we are shown in story form how inner attitudes produce outer states. Knowing the time when the animals would be ready for the act of creation and the watering hole to which they would come, Jacob made a bargain with his father-in-law that - although all of the animals were either black or brown, should any offspring be striped or spotted they would be his.

Believing man becomes what he beholds, and that the same would apply to the animal world, Jacob stripped the poplar trees so that only stripes appeared. Then he brought only the healthy animals to the watering hole, leaving all of the weak ones to breed - the brown with the brown and the black with the black. When the females came to the watering holes and were sired, they saw only stripes and producing what they beheld, their offsprings were striped.

So, this lesson was given us in the beginning. Whatever you are beholding in your mind's eye, you will produce in your outer world. It is just as simple as that. I hope you are beholding your fulfilled desire in your mind's eye; for scripture tells you that: "Whatever you desire, believe you have received it and you will." This is telling you that, to the degree you are self-persuaded, you will become what you have assumed you are.

In the case of my friend, his dream was telling him to continue to revise and not to be afraid of the responsibility of his tremendous power to imagine; for life itself is nothing more than an activity of imagination. When I speak of Christ being your life, I am saying he is your imagination, for life is an activity of imagination. Ask yourself what you are imagining right now and you will discover what Christ has created. For by him all things are created, and without him is not a thing created that is created.

Everything now formed and called a fact was once only an image in the mind of someone who persisted in that image and projected it onto the screen of space. So, do not give up the responsibility of revision, and - as to influencing others - may I say you cannot help it. As you walk the street you unwittingly influence people there. You simply cannot stop it.

Another point I want to bring up is this: The prophets who wrote the Old Testament were servants of the Lord. They recorded what they saw or heard, but they did not understand it. Every true prophet's vision is foreshortened. Seeing as present what is future: "The prophets prophesied of the grace that was to be yours. They searched and inquired as to what person or time was indicated by the Spirit of Christ within them when predicting the sufferings of Christ and the subsequent glory. It was revealed to them that they were serving, not themselves but you, in the things that are now being revealed."

Some of you are having wonderful visions and attempting to interpret them in this world. I urge you not to, as you will go astray when you try to determine an individual's departure - for no one knows the hour, day, or season. Only the Father knows and it remains his secret. It does not make any difference how perfect the vision, it was foreshortened. You saw it as taking place now. It may happen today or tomorrow, but you cannot foresee it. You saw the vision. Being a true prophet, record your visions in detail but do not attempt to interpret them.

That brings me to another point which has puzzled my friend. When I speak of God, or Lord, Jesus, or Christ, I am speaking of the human imagination. When asked to name the greatest of all commandments, he did not name one of the ten, but Israel's confession of faith saying: "Hear O Israel, the Lord our God, the Lord is one." The word "Lord" is JOD HE VAV HE (pron. "YOD HEY VAV HEY") meaning "I am". The word "God" is "Elohim" (pron. "e-lo-HEEM") which is a compound unity of one made up of many. In the 44th chapter of Ezekiel the Lord God said: "They shall have no inheritance; I AM their inheritance. Give them no possession; I AM their possession." Study this passage carefully and you will discover that instead of God inheriting us, we inherit God.

Greater love has no man than this: that he lay down his life for his friend. Not pretending, but voluntarily abandoning self for those he loved, God died that we may inherit him. What is He that we inherit?

He has told us "I AM the light of the world." One day you will inherit the experience of being the light of the universe. There will be no stars, no sun, no moon, no circumference - only infinite, pulsing, living light, which you know yourself to be. You will inherit God as infinite love. Whatever God was before he became individualized, you will experience as yourself.

God was a father before he became you and when he possesses you, you are the identical father. The 2nd Psalm reveals the son that was his before he became you. But no one knows who that son is except the Father, and no one knows who the Father is except that son and anyone to whom the son chooses to reveal him.

One day that son will choose to reveal you and you will see - not a David, but the David of Biblical fame. And there will be no uncertainty as to the relationship between you and God's son, David. When he calls you father, you will know that you are God.

When you inherit God, you inherit his infinite past, and from that moment on you will see scripture differently. You will recognize the events in the life of Jesus as signs of the initiative of God in man's redemption. You will understand how God gives himself to man.

John records eight signs of the initiative of God in Man's redemption. Many scholars have put the first and the last together, the second and the seventh, the third and the sixth and the fourth with the fifth, making four major signs. When these signs begin to unfold in you, count the days and you will discover there are 1260 days between the first vision and the last, as you inherit God.

You are not some little thing that God animates, gives life to, and owns. God gave himself to you in the ultimate sense of the word, so you shall have no inheritance, for I AM your inheritance. You shall have no possession in Israel, for I AM your possession. If you possess God, whatever He is, you must be!

I have just quoted the 44th chapter of Ezekiel. Read it carefully. Become aware of possessing God, and you will no longer be the little pygmy you were taught that you are. Don't react to the nonsense you read in the papers. They record the happenings of the surface mind.

What happens to a man between the cradle and the grave should not interest you. Whether he is a cook or a millionaire, the best-dressed man (or woman) of the year, or the most highly publicized - that's all relevant to this would and hasn't a thing to do with the Christ in you, who - as your life - will awaken one day and rise.

When Christ awoke in me I was so amazed, as I did not realize I had been asleep. Every morning I had awakened to a new day and retired that night, just as you have done throughout the ages. From the cradle to the grave you have fallen asleep at night and awakened in the morning. In time you have died, only to be restored to life to continue the same long journey. But one day you will awaken in the tomb where awareness was placed in the beginning. To your amazement you won't even remember falling asleep, and never for one second thought your skull was the tomb where they placed Jesus Christ.

But upon waking your inheritance will unfold, as everything said of Jesus Christ will be experienced by you in a first person, singular, present tense experience. You will discover you are the central actor in the divine drama of descent and ascent, for no one can ascend but he who descended.

Only Christ descended, so when you ascend you must be Christ. This is the hope that makes it wisdom to endure the suffering of this long dark night of time. Dwell upon that hope which is the grace that is coming to you at the unveiling of Christ in you, as you! There never was another and there never will be another, for Christ is your life!

Read the 3rd chapter, the 3rd and 4th verses of Colossians carefully. You have died and your life is hid with Christ in God. When Christ who is your life appears, you also shall appear with him in glory, because you are Christ! His appearance is his rising and awakening in you. His birth becomes your birth. The discovery of the fatherhood of God reveals you as the father, and the 44th chapter of Ezekiel is fulfilled. I AM your inheritance! I AM your possession!

Remember: everything you see, although it appears on the outside it is within you. You do not have to be concerned about influencing individuals if you make goals. If you want a great deal of money, see the money within you. Then claim it is yours!

Today a very rich man is getting a great deal of publicity because of his marriage. Born a poor boy in Turkey of Greek parents, he was taken to Argentina when he was sixteen, where he began to import tobacco, starting his business with sixty dollars. He has completely forgotten those days, and the one he would marry - because of ambition for greatness in name - would have you forget his lowly beginnings. Shakespeare had a word for it: "He denies the ladder by which he did ascend." Starting with sixty dollars, this man began to dream and today he is a billionaire. I would not ask him how he stole it. So far, he has gotten away with it and it is considered his, but anyone with a billion dollars must have stolen it. It doesn't matter however, as all things work for good in the end.

It should not matter what a man does with his life between the cradle and the grave. The important thing is what is happening within the man. Has the life that animates that body been stirred? Is it beginning to rise in him? It must rise in order to inherit God, for only Christ inherits God. Christ is your life which must rise in you, and when he does you inherit God the Father.

Whether you play the part of a cook or a king, a carpenter or movie idol, is not important - for your external state means nothing. There are men who are now playing the part of a cook, carpenter, shoeshine boy, or barber, knowing they are redeemed, waiting patiently for that moment in time when they can take off the garment of flesh and blood for the last time. But only the Father knows that moment. Let no one speculate as to when it will happen. Record your visions, but do not interpret them. We are all past masters at misinterpretation of the great mission of God to us.

As for me, I have already risen. I am of the world, not in it. My dreams and experiences at night are not related to this world, so I play a double life. While I am here there is work to be done to continue to encourage everyone by telling the true story of redemption.

Take this wonderful story to heart. It is a true one. Christ is your life which is wholly supernatural. The birth is supernatural. The discovery of the Father is supernatural. The tearing of the temple from top to bottom and the ascent into the kingdom are supernatural, as well as the descent of the dove. No physical dove descends upon your shoulder - it is a supernatural experience, but this fantastic truth has been embodied in a tale that man could understand; for, as Tennyson said: "Truth embodied in a tale shall enter in at lowly doors."

Remember what I have said. Forget influence! Take objectives. Conceive a scene which would imply the fulfillment of your desire and dream noble dreams, for nothing is impossible to Christ and Christ is your life!

Now let us go into the silence.

Christic Unveiled

onight's subject is "Christ Unveiled." That is quite a tall order, for we are told in Mark 13:21: "If anyone says to you, 'Look, here is Christ!' or 'Look, there he is!' do not believe it." And I will endorse that one hundred percent. Listen to it carefully and see the pronoun used in that sentence. "Here he is, believe him not." So, here, who is Christ? What is Christ? Where is Christ? Paul found him and, having found him, he said: "From now on we regard no one from a human point of view even though we once regarded Christ from a human point of view, we regard him thus no longer."[3] He regards him not, from now on, as man. He thought he was man and went out to destroy those who believed in Christ as a man.

Then we are told in I Peter 1:10,11: "The prophets who prophesied of the grace that was to be yours searched and inquired about this salvation; they inquired what person or time was indicated by the Spirit of Christ within them when predicting the sufferings of Christ and the subsequent glory." They thought they were looking for a person, or time, and they wondered whether he would come. There was no reply to that, save "It was revealed to them they were serving not themselves but you" (v. 12) What is Christ? I tell you Christ is "The Way" of salvation. Christ is "The Way" to the Father.

Now we will turn back to the Gospels where we have these events together, for Scripture, as we understand it, says the New Testament is based on the affirmation that a certain series of events happened in which God revealed himself in action for the salvation of man. Did they happen? I tell you from experience, they happened. Not only they happened, but are happening. They are taking place every moment of time in our world. If you have not experienced these events may I tell you: you are going to. Not a thing in this world that

---

[3] 1 Cor. 5:16

you will ever do will stop it. God will not fail - not in one being in this world. Here we are told the events were assembled and Luke, in his first four verses, makes the statement: "Inasmuch as many have undertaken to compile a narrative of the things which have been accomplished among us, just as they were delivered to us by those who from the beginning were eyewitnesses and ministers of the word, it seemed good to me also, having followed all things for some time past, to write an orderly account for you, most excellent Theophilus, that you may know the truth concerning the things of which you have been informed." So, here we have the oral tradition. They all talked about it. These things happened and they are telling it, but come the moment in time that many undertook to put it into written form and he thought it wise to do the same thing. And so, he said: "Having observed all things closely for some time past." He thought he, too, would put it in written form for one he called Theophilus - meaning "one who loves God." He is speaking to you. You love God, I love God. He is the source of everything - the source of our life and the end of all things. And, so, he is addressing his remarks to you - O dear Theophilus - that you may know the truth concerning the things of which you have been informed.

And so, we heard it orally. I did as a child, but when I began to read and write I could read it for myself, but did not understand it. Before I could read it, mother taught it to me and I was sent to school and it was taught to me in school. Then I was sent to Sunday school and I heard the story told by the teacher. And, so, we heard it orally. Then came the moment in time we could read it for ourselves. Then came this closed book.

Now, let us see if we can unveil Christ tonight. In Matthew 16:13, one called Christ Jesus turns to his disciples and asked this question: "Who do men say that the Son of man is?" And they replied, "Some say John the Baptist, others say Elijah, and others Jeremiah or one of the prophets." Then he said to them: "But who do you say that I am?" Right away that second question identifies it with the son of man. The first question is: "But who do you say that I am?" So he is asking the question about the Son of Man. Then he is asking about himself. "But who do you say that I am?" He identifies himself with the Son of Man. And Peter replied: "You are the Christ, the Son of the living God." And to this he answered: "Blessed are you, Simon bar Jonah! For flesh and blood has not revealed this to you, but my Father who is in heaven." He confesses that no flesh and blood could have told it, it has to come by revelation. Where do we find this flesh and blood revelation? In Galatians 1:16, 17. "When it pleased God to reveal His son in me, I conferred not with flesh and blood." That, mortal mind could not reveal, no matter how it rationalized or tried to unravel this mystery. It cannot, it has to be revealed - it has to be completely unfolded, in the individual. So, he said: "I am the Son of man."

Now, we go back in the Old Testament to find this cue. Where did God promise this? We turn to 2 Samuel, 7th Chapter. This is a vision. We are told between the 8th and 17th verses, that Nathan received a vision, and "according to all these words and according to all this vision, Nathan spoke to David. This is what he told David: "And the Lord said unto me - the Lord of Hosts O go to my servant David and say to David, 'When your days are fulfilled and you lie down with your fathers, I will raise up your son after you, who shall come forth from your body, and I will be his father, and he shall be my son.' Here, we have to now spiritualize the vision of David. Here is David, a man. If "I will raise up your son after you," then he is David's son. I cannot deny it. "I will raise up your son after you who will come forth from your body." "I will (now the Lord is speaking) be his father and he shall be my son." If he is the son of David then he is the Son of man. If, on the other hand, the Lord adopts him, "He shall be my son," then he is the Son of God. So, in this case, who do men say the Son of man is? And they all thought of all kinds of things. He said then: "Who do you say I am?" "You are Christ, the Son of God." Now right away you think in terms "You are Christ, the Son of God" and yet - the Son of man, you think of a man. And it is not so at all.

Here is a man as you are - male or female - walking the earth. You have heard the story orally, but when you began to read you could read it for yourself, but you did not understand it. You are playing your normal part in this world and one day when you least expect it - in fact, you never expect it - you thought it happened 2,000 years ago to one person and that was it - well, you are that person. It is happening to you. You go through the entire series of events as recorded in Scripture, and then you know who Christ is. Christ is "The Way" to the Father - and there is no other Way. "I am the Way." To what? To everything in this world! But especially to the Father. "I am the Way. No one comes unto the Father but by me," as told in the 14th chapter of John. But no one comes unto the Father but by me." So, here is the Way. What is the Way? Then you search the Scripture and find the Way, and the Way you do not determine - it was in the beginning. Listen to the statement carefully, in Paul's Letter to the Colossians (1:15-17): "He is the image of the invisible God, the first-born of all creation; for in him all things were created, in heaven and on earth, visible and invisible, whether thrones or dominions or principalities or authorities - all things were created through him for him. He is before all things, and in him all things hold together."

"He is the image of the invisible God - the first born of all creation." Now where is this said in the Old Testament? Because the New is only the fulfillment. The whole is in the Old and the New is fulfillment. You will find it in Proverbs 8:22, 23: "The Lord created me at the beginning of his work, the first of his acts of old. Ages ago I was set up, at the first, before the beginning of the earth . . . when he marked out the foundations of the earth, then I was beside him like a little child." (*v. 29*) Here is God's way of salvation. But God's way in Scripture is always personified. Every attribute of man's mind, which is God's mind, is always personified. If it is wealth, you see wealth as a man. If it is power, you see power as a man. When you meet Infinite Might - it is a man. All the attributes of mind are always personified, for God is man and man is God. So He personifies this Way - the Way that was in the beginning. This is not improvised. Before God brought the whole vast world into being, he plotted and planned a way of redemption for all of us. This is not an afterthought of God. It came first. "I am the first of his acts of old," before he brought forth the world - the universe, anything - he planned a Way, and the Way was to God, personified as a little child. "And I was daily his delight, rejoicing before him always, rejoicing in his inhabited world and delighting in the sons of man."[4]

Now listen carefully: "He who finds me finds life and obtains favor from the Lord; but he who misses me injures himself; all who hate me love death."[5] Where is it in the New Testament - the second part of what we just quoted? The very first words uttered by Jesus recorded in Scripture you will find in the last few verses in Luke 2. It takes place in the synagogue - the temple - and his parents said to him: "Son, why have you treated us so? Behold, your father and I have been looking for you anxiously." And he replied: "How is it that you sought me? Did you not know that I must be in my Father's house?" And they did not understand the saying which he spoke to them." But, the mother kept these things in her heart, and then Jesus grew in years, in wisdom, and in the favor of the Lord. The first recorded utterance of Jesus in Scripture when he was only a lad, a child: "Did you not know that I must be in my Father's house?" He said heaven is the throne of God and heaven is within you. Where would you find him? You are asking me? Where would you seek me? They sought him elsewhere, but they could not find him until they found him in the father's house - for you are the temple of the living God. It is called synagogue, outwardly. You are the synagogue, but you are the temple of the living God. I will not find the way until I find him myself. And find him without searching for him. One day when it pleases God - for it comes with the fullness of time and he sees in me the ripeness he is looking for - then he unfolds me by this series of events, in his home.

First the birth, then the discovery of his son, and then the splitting of the temple. And I am taken into his home - and his home is within. Just as described in the 13th Chapter of Mark, there is the

---

[4] Proverbs 8:30, 31
[5] Prov. 8:35, 36

most frightening earthquake when you are taken into his home, and you are the cause of it. When you move up and move into that heavenly state within you, there is a vibration you have never experienced before. The whole vast world within you begins to shake because you have been redeemed. You are brought in and there is joy beyond the wildest dream you could ever conceive, because one more has been brought into the temple, into the house of God.

It is true as I have told you. So, Christ is the Way, the Way of redemption, and the Way is man. "The Lord created me at the beginning of His Way, the first of his acts of old." Before he brought forth the stars or anything, he created a way of return to himself, and that way is called Christ in the Bible. And the people sought him and the prophets inquired as to what person, and to this day, in 1963, they are still looking for a person. You will see it in the papers - they are always looking for some person coming into the world that will be Christ and they are so eager to find a Christ on the outside. They thought they found one in Hitler, or in Stalin, or someone else - always a savior of the world. But, as quoted earlier from Mark 13:21: "And then if anyone says to you, 'Look here is the Christ!' or 'Look, there he is!' do not believe it." You will never find him in another. In no being in this world will you find him. You either find him in yourself as the Way that leads you to God, or you will not find him. But you will find him - everyone will find him. And when they find him, they find him as a "Way." He said: "I am the Way, I am the Truth, I am the Life; I am the Resurrection; I am the Door." There is no other door. You cannot get through it in any other way, and this is the Way of the Father. The Way is inwoven in every child in this world and that child will find the way when God is ready for him, for only God knows that moment in eternity when he will awaken that child.

Now, why are we called in 2 Samuel 7: "Those who sleep with the Fathers?" Here we are three billion in the world today, and "When your days are fulfilled and you lie down with your fathers, I will raise up your son after you, who shall come forth from your body, and I will establish his kingdom." And you think those were the fathers. May I tell you: you are the fathers. You have already fulfilled your day in preparation, and now you are sleeping with the fathers. You are sound asleep, but you don't know it. You came here tonight as a conscious being and you will go home tonight - drive your cars or get off the bus at the right points, you will go to bed fully conscious of the fact that this is when you are going to sleep and that prior to that you were awake. You did all these things conscious.

I have observed my brother Bruce; from the time he was born he was a sleep walker. Bruce would come down stairs and go to the larder, unlock the larder for some milk and bread and jam. He would walk around naturally. We would do everything to make him fall on his neck, but he never did. He walked around the chairs or anything else in the room and then came back upstairs and went back to bed, totally unaware he had done anything unnatural, and the only person in the world who could convince him he did it was my mother. He would oppose us, but not mother. Not that she would have done anything violent, but he could not mistrust my mother. She was to us the ideal. She would not lie to us. So our brother Bruce trusted her, but he would rack his brain to find out why he did it. We put obstacles in his way but he would walk around them.

That taught me a lesson in my mature years when I was awakened to find that I had been asleep all through the ages and I did not know it. All through the ages I have been sleeping - and how long are these ages? Paul tells us in his letter to the Colossians, "The mystery hidden for ages and generations . . . which is Christ in you, the hope of glory."[6] He tells us a mystery - the mystery - the mystery is Christ in us, the hope of glory. I did not understand it any more than the world understands it, and one day it happened. And God, in his infinite mercy, looked upon me and found me ripe, and he woke me. I awoke for the first time in eternity, and I was sealed in a tomb, and the tomb was my skull. And God rolled away the stone and I came out. But

---

[6] Col. 1:26, 27

until that moment I never thought for one moment I was asleep. Not only asleep, but the sleep was so deep, so profound, I was dead. For when I awoke I was in a tomb, and you do not put anyone in a tomb unless they are dead. So, when you enter that tomb you are dead, and you are one with Christ, who died for you. He is the Way. Together you are completely sealed in a tomb. But you don't know it. I did not know it. But I have never been more awake in eternity. When I saw things around about me and saw them all objectively, and they could not see me, I understood the words: "He is the image of the Invisible God." How could you be the image of something invisible? But those are the words: "The image of the invisible God" - the first of all that was created. How could I actually reflect something invisible? It was true, you are the image of the invisible God and nothing that is mortal that looks at you can see you. You are more real than anything in the world. And the whole thing began to come back and I began to see the experiences I have come through and I wondered, for it puzzled me. Looking at you - looking at myself, bathing, shaving, taking care of the body, and it seemed so alive and so independent of any man's perception of it. I could leave the room when I wanted to and do the things I wanted to do but at this moment in time I realized this is not so at all.

When I awoke, I then realized an experience I had many years before. God was bringing me to that point of awakening. In one moment in time he took me into a world just like this and showed me a power that would be myself tomorrow. He allowed me to exercise it just for a moment and I saw people just like you. As I saw them, I arrested within myself a rhythm - an action. As I did it, the people I observed stood still - everything stood still. I wondered how it could be, but they could not move. But when I released the activity within me that I arrested, they all moved on and completed their intention. Then it broke. Then I understood what he meant: "As the Father has life within himself, so he has granted to the son to have life in himself."

So, everyone is destined to have life within himself. Then you wonder about these garments and all these things round about us - this thing called Neville. What are all these things? Are these really costumes? Is something being formed in us that is the image of the Invisible God and we have to play these parts and wear these costumes for the moment? I have concluded that it is true - that, as Shakespeare says, the whole vast world is really a stage and all men are merely the players. And one man plays many parts in his time, and the being playing it all is God - individualizing himself and begetting himself, as told in 2 Samuel 7: "I will raise up your son after you, who shall come forth from your body. I will be his father and he shall be my son." Out of this human body something is coming forward that is going to be called the Son of man, because it comes out of man. But it will be the Son of God, and it is the image of the Invisible God - something born in man and he brings him forward. And may I tell you: it is your own sense of I-ness. No loss of identity when you are awakened. None whatsoever. You will know me in eternity and I will know you.

But for all the sameness of identity, we will know each other. But there is going to be a radical discontinuity of form - a radical discontinuity. You have no idea how beautiful you really are. Human face, yes. Human hands, yes. Human feet, yes. The human body - no. Not this body, not for one moment, but I cannot describe it to you. Not that I wouldn't, if I could, but I can't. If I made an attempt, it could only be radiant light, like a rainbow. Yet I would know you and you will know me, for there is a sameness of identity and human enough we can recognize each other. But the form - a radical discontinuity. You can display it and you know who you are, then you return to this - this garment, that you will one day put down forever, and this is essential.

Before this came into being, God mapped out a way, and The Way was called Christ. No one understood who Christ was. They thought it was a man who would come and save the world. (People are always looking for a man that will come and save the world.) That man is you. You are David. He brings forward your son, but that is his son. Then you will understand the great opening statement of Matthew: "The book of the genealogy of Jesus Christ, the son of David, the son of Abraham." Then he brings up the question, "What think ye of the Christ; whose son is he?" The question is not complete until you listen to the past part - "son of David." "Then why did David, in Spirit, call him father?" And you will see the Son of man is also the Son of God. But the Son of God and God are one. "I and my Father are one." You get it? I and my Father are one, and yet I am the Son of man.

This is man, and out of man comes a being that is God's son. And then David - who played this fantastic part, which is now universal humanity - becomes the Son of man. You follow it? The Son of man is one with the Son of God. But that out of which the Son of man comes (who is the Son of God) in turn becomes the Son of man. You follow it? Son of man - Son of God - God. The Son of God and God are one, if the Son of God cannot deny the product of man.

The question is asked in the 16th chapter of Matthew: "Who do men say the Son of man is?" Naturally, because He is the Son of man they have to think in terms of man, and they say: "Some say John the Baptist, others say Elijah, and others Jeremiah or one of the prophets." So they mention man. He does not quarrel with that. He changes it, now: "But who do you say that I am?" He is asking: "Who is I?" He tells you: "I am the son of man - but who am I?" They mention "the Christ, the Son of the living God." Then he tells them; "Flesh and blood has not revealed this to you, but my Father who is in Heaven." Then he comes down to the foundation - who is the Son of man? The Son of God? God? It comes out David. That is the promise given to us.

David is collective humanity, and out of David comes the Son of man and that Son of Man is the Son of God. When the Son of God awakes, he has to have a son, and it is David. Jesus never got beyond that age of 12 where he appears in the temple, and they ask: "Where were you? We have been looking all over for you. Why did you do this unto us? And He says: "Why did you seek me? You found me in my

Father's house. Why did you seek me elsewhere. You can't find me, but if you find me you find life and receive the favor of the Lord."

When you find life, you will do to everyone in this world what it has been my privilege to do. In these moments I was taken, in the Spirit, and put into sections of humanity and stopped them. Then I released it, and they completed their action. And I stopped them again and they could go no further. A bird. A leaf. And then you ask fantastic questions in the depths of your soul. And you come to the conclusion that this whole vast world - everything in it - is a resultant state of God's first creative act, and this was brought into being as a resultant state, and you are not these garments of flesh at all. Something is being formed in this garment of flesh. What is being formed? It is called the Son of man, but God calls it his Son, and his Son and himself are one. So God is begetting himself in man - his very own Self - and the day will come the individual will be able to say to himself; "He is not only begetting his Son, he begot his son in me, and I and my Father are one." When you are awakened there is no other being but you and you, yourself, awake in yourself to discover you have been sound asleep and really dead for these unnumbered ages.

So when he tells you in his Letter to the Colossians: "The mystery hidden for ages and generations . . . which is Christ in you, the hope of glory," there is a way in man that leads him to glory. But man does not know it. He thinks he is completely awake and independent. I can go back 30 years ago and I would walk on Broadway, and it happened often. I was young and strong. Not a thing was wrong with me, and yet I would walk up Broadway and all of a sudden I knew someone was arresting me and I could not walk. And I would stop in the street and I could not put one foot in front of the other, but I did not understand it, and I would be released and walk on. Then it would happen again - on the sidewalk. I could not move, and I was fully alert and conscious, but I was still. And I know, now, someone was doing to me then what I, years later, was taken in Spirit to do to others. I was being trained and prepared to do the same thing to another that was done to me. I could not move. And yet, I was playing on Broadway. I had my vaudeville shows and played everything east of the Mississippi. I was a professional dancer and nothing was wrong with me and, yet, I could not move. I could feel something holding me - not embracing me - but something binding me. I stood paralyzed. And after a minute or so, whatever it was released me. I was used as the guinea pig by someone using this power within himself as I, years later, used it on others.

So, "As the Father has life in Himself, so he grants the Son also to have life in himself," and he is about to awaken that son and he knows it. We are being ripened - we must all conform to the image of the invisible God. When the image is coming into view, he introduces that being to the power that he will exercise tomorrow, so he takes him in spirit and shows him this fabulous world and he has control over it.

What is the world? It is a stage, but you are not the garment you are wearing. But I will recognize you. There is a sameness of identity and we will know everyone in eternity. But there is a radical discontinuity of form. So, this body of ours - face, hands, feet - yes. But not the body. You are beautiful beyond your wildest dream!

Now let us go into the silence.

Q & A

Question: The Bible speaks of perfect love casting out all fear.

Answer: If you came into a world, and you could multiply this to encompass the entire world - but should you come into a place, say, as large as this room, with an audience like this, and suddenly you knew in the depths of your soul that you, by stilling - not them, but stilling an activity in yourself, everyone would be stilled; and you did it and proved the truth of your intuition - who then could disturb you? If you were faced now with the most horrible thing in the world and you by stilling an activity in yourself made it still, and it is so still it could outlast marble; if you didn't release that activity in yourself you wouldn't have to embalm it, it wouldn't decay, it would stand just as it is.

Suppose you were faced with an army of millions, armed to the teeth, but they were earthly minded, and then you stilled the activity in you that gave them motion. And suppose in you, you could change their intention or direction. You could by changing their direction march them into the ocean and when they got beyond sight, you released the activity within you, then what would happen to them? They would be once more flesh and blood and they would drown. Do you know that? But you wouldn't do that, because you would not be afraid of man and they are only men.

So, all this is processing that God is extracting his sons from man. It is from man; therefore, it is man's son. "I will raise up your son after you who shall come forth from your body, but I will be his father and he shall be my son." So, God is begetting his son in man, bringing him out of man; but he can't deny he is a man therefore he is man's son. It is man's offspring but it is God's son now, for this is going to be done differently. This that comes from the world, my son, comes from the womb of my wife; but when my son in this world came from the womb of his mother, he is brought forth from that body. He will also be brought forth from his skull. That is the second birth. There are two births; one is from the womb of woman and one is from the skull of man. That is the second reaching forth from the skull, - that is God's son.

Now the question is asked in the Book of Timothy: "And how will woman be saved?" Because man does not quite understand generic man. The answer is wrongly translated. "Woman will be saved by the bearing of the child." Unfortunately, they put that in the foot-note and they gave as the answer: "Woman will be saved by bearing children." It hasn't a thing to do with any bearing of children. "Woman will be saved by the bearing of the child," just as man is saved. But they can't believe that man could bear a child. He can sire one but he can't bear one. Yet the question is asked in the Book of Jeremiah: "Can man have a child, can he bear a child?" The question is not answered but God answers it by stating that he is seeing, having asked the question. "Can a man bear a child? Why then do I see every man with his hands delivering himself, pulling himself out of himself just like a woman in labor."[7] And in the 2nd Chapter of Timothy: "How then will woman be saved?" and I tell you the true translation of that phrase is "By the bearing of the child." The foot note uses it and they tell you the literal Greek is "Bearing of the child." But they cannot understand it any more than they could understand Jeremiah, so they say: "Woman will be saved by bearing children." It hasn't a thing to do with bearing children. Salvation does it entirely differently - out of the skull of generic man, male or female. The symbolism is the first step in the great Way called Christ. Christ is the way, and the first step is the birth of the individual by being resurrected, symbolized in the birth of a child.

They find the sign they were told they would find when this event takes place in eternity. They will find the sign and the sign is the child, and they will tell you it is your child. They will give it to you and you will hold it, as told in the Book of Luke, and you will have a joy in the Way of salvation.

There is a definite way and there is no other way. People say: "Well, there must be another way." I swear there is no other way. Foundation is the only salvation. Don't try to get away from it. It is the only foundation. It is all in the Hebraic world as a promise. So, it is said: "He opened unto thee the Scriptures and they said within themselves: "'Did not our hearts burn when he opened to us the Scripture,' and beginning with Moses and all through the prophets and the Psalms he interprets to them all concerning himself." The whole thing is about himself — that is, you. Moses rejoiced. He rejoiced for what? "He endured all the fires of Egypt; he gave up all the treasures of Egypt, because he considered the wealth of Christ far greater, and he endured as seeing him who is invisible." He endured. Read the story of Moses. How would you say that Moses, who preceded him by thousands of years, endured as seeing him? That is told in the 11th

---

[7] Jeremiah 30

chapter of the Book of Hebrews: "Moses endured as seeing him who is invisible."

Now we are told that "Abraham rejoiced that he was to see my day. He saw it and was glad." How could Abraham rejoice? Everything was in preparation and then came that moment in time when the first could be brought forward, but from that moment on all are being brought forward. How many in the world? I don't know, but all are being brought forward and not one will fail. So, what is doing it? "He who began a good work in you will bring it to completion at the day of Jesus Christ." So, the day is coming when that moment in time you are the image of that invisible God, God is bringing forth. He can't bring you forth until you conform to the image of the invisible God, for you must be one with your Father. That you are one with him in the true essence of the word: "I and my Father are one."

Christmas - Man's Birth *as* God

"In the beginning was the Word and the Word was with God and the Word was God. The Word became flesh and dwells in us."[8] Our physical birth is God's incarnation, for incarnation signifies the assumption by a divine being of human or animal form. When you were born your little human form was assumed by God. Christmas marks the departure from God's incarnation and your birth as God.

There are two births: one when God assumes your human form and the other when you assume the divine form as God! The first birth is from below, while the second birth - called Christmas - is from above. Every child born of woman is God incarnate, or the child could not be aware that he is. His consciousness is God's incarnation. The world, not knowing this, celebrates the wrong event; for Christmas is when man becomes conscious of being God.

Here are a few paradoxes which disturb many people. All of these are actual quotes or interpretations of a quote:

> *"I shall no longer speak to you in figures, but tell you plainly of the Father."*
>
> *"I came out from the Father and came into the world. Again I am leaving the world and going to the Father."*
>
> *"I and my Father are one."*
>
> *"I am going to the Father, for the Father is greater than I."*
>
> *"When you see me, you have seen the Father."*
>
> *"He who you call God, he is my Father, but I know my Father and you know not your God."*
>
> *"Show us the Father. If you knew me you would not ask, for no one can know me in the true sense and not know God, for He and I are inseparable."*

---

[8] John 1

66

Who is the father who is one with his son, yet greater than he? Can he be the son of God, yet God the Father? And how can I ever know that I and my Father are one? Let us try to solve these strange contradictions.

In the last chapter of the Book of Revelation, God says: "I am the root and the offspring of David, the bright morning star." God is the root, the source, the cause of all life. He is the father of David, yet his offspring!

As the source God is David's father, called Jesse or I AM. As the offspring David is called the son of God. The prophet Samuel spoke to David, saying: "God declared that when your days are fulfilled, and you lie down with your fathers, I will raise up your son after you who will come forth from your body. I will be his father and he shall be my son."[9]

Here we see that the root and the offspring are one. I (the root of David) am the cause of all life. In spite of that I come out of David, recognize him and say: "Thou art my son, today I have begotten thee."

As God the Father, I assume the limitations of the flesh; and using one who is a man after my heart and will do all my will, I become conscious of being a rich man, a poor man, a beggar, and a thief, until David reveals me as his father. "I came to do the will of my Father yet I am the Father, for God the Father and the Son of God is one I AM."

There is only God in the world. As the father God created a perfect play. As the son God plays all the parts. As the son God is restricted in his activities. But when the drama is finished God leaves the world of Caesar - greatly expanded - and returns to himself, the Father.

As the son God suffers. Ask a man who is suffering and he will answer, I am! That's the Father, who has become incarnate by assuming human form. When the play is over for him, God will leave the world as the son, to return to the kingdom of heaven as the Father. In our mystery this event is called Christmas. Your entrance

---

[9] II Samuel 7

into this world is God's incarnation. His departure occurs when his promise to himself is fulfilled in you and you experience a wonderful series of mystical events.

Like Paul, I pray that those who believe my message of salvation will know it is true; that the name I gave them for God is not mere poetry, but fact - that you are the Father. I have told them what happened in me. Grant them to know it is true. I am sure my departure will quicken the pace for those who have heard, accepted, and believed my words.

Now, a gentleman wrote, saying: "I fell asleep and dreamed I was reading the newspaper, looking at a full-page advertisement for Western Airlines. They were announcing their new P.D. system, which would eliminate all passenger congestion when boarding the plane. Suddenly the page became animated and I am in the picture, grinning from ear to ear as I awoke." In his letter he wondered why the initials P.D. He thought the D could be for departure, but could not understand the P. although he used the word "plan" throughout his letter.

Everything contains within itself the capacity for symbolic significance. This gentleman is in advertising so naturally, in the dream he is looking at an ad. In this modern world we have planes which take man from earth to the skies and bring him back again. But this is a plan of transportation.

In the Book of Ephesians, we read: "He has made known unto us the mystery of his will in all wisdom and insight according to his purpose which he set forth as a plan in Christ for the fullness of time to unite all things in him, things in heaven and things on earth."

My friend called it the departure. This does not necessarily mean that he goes tonight or in the next forty years. To me as the interpreter of the dream it means that he has finished the journey. Like Paul, the time for his departure has come. He has fought the good fight. He has finished the race and kept the faith. Henceforth, there is laid up for him the crown of righteousness.

This crown is not something filled with jewels, but is the victor's crown. Only when one has finished the race can the crown be given. He has fought his own battle with himself, and he has won. His flight into the heavens is a plan which will erupt, causing him to depart this world of Caesar to personally experience Christmas.

Christmas is not the incarnation of God, but the departure of Man as God; for God became Man that Man may become God. In my friend's dream he took the images of the twentieth century, and since everything contains within itself the capacity for symbolic significance, an airplane symbolizes that which takes off towards the heavens. It's destined to rise above the earth. The "P" is the plan of departure which begins with a spiritual birth, followed by the revelation of man's true identity.

There is no way of knowing who you really are until God's Son reveals it, for "No one knows who the Son is except the Father, and no one knows who the Father is except the son and anyone to whom the Son chooses to reveal him." The Son must choose to reveal you, for only then do you know you are God the Father.

I am the way. I am the truth. I am the light. No one comes to the awareness of being the Father except by God's plan. Diet will not do it. Wearing certain clothes, hibernating in some so-called holy place, or being a priest and going up the ranks will not do it. There is only one way to the Father, and I - all imagination - am the way!

My friend is a happily married man with three children, yet he is so hungry for the truth; so I say: Father, let the truth of my words be known, that he and all those who believe my words know that the love with which thou has loved me may be in them, and I in them.

One day you will discover that God - the Father who became you - has completed his work. And because he was God when he became you, when his work is complete you will become aware that you are God. There is only one way to know this for a fact, and that is when God's son, David, stands before you and reveals you as his father. Then the temple of the Living God - which is spirit - is split in two, and you ascend into heaven as a fiery serpent. And finally, the symbol of the Holy Spirit in the form of a dove descends, and - clothing you with Himself - once more sends you back into this world, to tell your story to those who will listen.

This gentleman had a wonderful dream. He may someday devise a plan that Western Airlines will use to ease the boarding congestion, but that was not the message of the dream. He is departing this world of Caesar. Having already had these experiences, he has forgotten them. But he will remember and know that when the time comes for him to depart this little section of time, he will not be restored to life, but will enter the New Age. Being one with the body of God he will know no restrictions, only the complete freedom of being God the Father.

Having entered the world, God the Father of all life incarnated himself in your flesh and blood body as the son. When God's work is complete, He will depart this body and return to his heavenly body as the Father, redeeming you. This is the way to redemption, and there is no other way.

Although the words, "I and my father are one, yet my father is greater than I" appear to be contradictory, they are true. When I - the awareness - take on the limitation of flesh, I am aware of limitation. Finding myself in the form of a slave, I become obedient until death upon the cross called Man, where I remain as God, restricted by my incarnation. Then a predetermined plan erupts and delivers me from my self-imprisonment, and I return to the being I was - but now enhanced because of my self-imposed restriction. Then I can say with Paul: "I have fought the good fight. I have finished the race. I have kept the faith. Now there is laid up for me the laurel leaf - the crown of righteousness."

I am reminded of a story told of Charles William Eliot, who - when he retired as president of Harvard University - was given a gift by an old friend in Boston which he treasured greatly. His friend sent him an envelope containing a single laurel leaf. Its message was clear. He was being told he was victorious. Everyone will eventually receive that crown of righteousness, as the same crown is given to all who come to the end of the journey.

Coming out from the awareness of being God the Father, you came into the world, becoming aware of being Man. You are predestined to return to the awareness of being God the Father once more. This is the story of Man.

God comes into the world by assuming human form. He incarnates himself at the birth of a child in order for it to breathe. While here God goes through literal hell, because his life does not end with the grave. Making his exit from this world of death, God is restored to life to continue the journey; to die and be restored once more, over and over again, until he finds this series of supernatural events which leads God to his home - and Christmas.

Christmas marks the birth of man as God, not the birth of God as man. There is all the difference in the world. Matthew and Luke tell the story of the birth, not as a little physical child, but as a sign of an individual's birth as God, for God is born that day in the city of David.

When God is born in you it will be in the city of David. At that moment you are born as God. And from then on you will grow in stature. You will grow in favor of the Father because you will know yourself to be one with him. You will continue to remain incarnate, however, until that moment when you express your last breath. Then you will discover yourself to be life itself, for you will have entered the one body, one Spirit, one Lord, one God and Father of all.

Once individuality became defused in all, as told us in the 82nd Psalm: "I say, 'You are gods, sons of the Most High, all of you; nevertheless, you will die like men and fall as one man, O princes.' "Here is this universal diffusion of the one I AM. You say, I am. I say, I am. We say, I am. That's the one being who fell, incarnating himself by becoming Man.

I don't care what is said about Buddha's or Confucius' way; I have told you the only way back to the Father. My testimony is not based upon theory, but upon my own personal experience, and I tell you a truth: there is only one way. I am the way!

Another gentleman (an artist by profession) wrote, saying: "I found myself at the bottom of a deep well. Looking up I could see a beautiful blue sky with little clusters of white clouds which became doves, with their wings spread as though floating. Then I said to myself: 'This is what Neville teaches. The dove really does float'."

I am thrilled that in this man's dream, he recalled the teaching. In the Book of Genesis, we are told that when the flood of illusion is over, the dove appears bringing back the laurel leaf (*sic*): the sprig of victory. And the dove actually floats upon the crystal-clear water.

I have seen this great flood of illusion as crystal clear atmosphere and now know that for me, the ark, the flood, is over. Man is either the ark of God or a phantom of the earth and sea - and he is not a phantom! Man is the ark of God, containing everything within himself.

Recently a great doctor was asked about the flu which is spreading all over our country. Questioning where the bug goes when the flu subsides, he answered: "It doesn't go anywhere. It remains in man to be activated again." I say moods activate it.

Leprosy doesn't come from without. Cancer doesn't either. Everything is within man. Read the paper and react. That reaction sets a feeling in motion, be it anger, frustration, or irritation. When the feeling leaves, where does it go? Back to sleep within you, for you contain the world and all that is in it.

God became you and, containing all, God is absolute. The world teaches that God is all good and never evil. But if there is evil, and God is not evil, then God is not absolute.

If you can experience something that God cannot then you must be greater than God, and that is not possible. When you read of an innocent boy who was murdered and you react, you activate something within you. It may be tomorrow's tooth or stomach ache. I do not know what it will be, but God is not mocked. As you sow a reaction you reap an act, for you and God are one.

God actually became as you are the moment you breathed, for breath and spirit are one and the same word in Hebrew and Greek. When you were spanked on the behind, took one deep inhalation and breathed, God became incarnate in you. Then you go through the furnaces of experience to reach the end, when you experience this series of events. No other event or events will take you back.

The first event is your awakening and resurrection from the skull where God entered. Then your birth as God. Coming out of your skull, all of the symbolism of scripture as described in Matthew and Luke is before you.

The three witnesses are there, as well as the child wrapped in swaddling clothes. The witnesses talk about you, but cannot see you, as you are now spirit.

Then, because no one has ever seen God but his only begotten son who is in the bosom of the Father, the second event occurs, when God's son stands before you and makes you known to yourself. Then you, too, will say: "I am the root and the offspring of David." For, coming out of the garment you have worn throughout your journey in the world of death, you are David, God's only begotten son!

There is no other way back to the realization of being God the Father, for He literally became you that you may become God. We are told that Jesus Christ is God's son, yet it is he who claims: I and my Father are one. He who sent me has seen the Father. Claiming to be the son who is the Father is a paradox; yet it is resolved when you realize that the son - coming out from the Father - remains the Father, but is restricted by incarnation.

God the Father takes upon himself the form of a slave, and - becoming the son - he is obedient until death, even death upon the cross of Man. This God wears, as He moves from one state to another, to another in what the world calls death, until God experiences the one definite plan to return to himself - the Father. So, Christmas marks, not the incarnation of God, but the birth of man, as God.

Now let us go into the silence.

Conception

onight's subject is on conception, both on this level and the highest level. The Bible is vision from beginning to end. Words such as Jesus, Moses, Abraham, and Isaac are used, but their stories are visions. Jesus is the fulfillment of scripture, so when I speak of Jesus, I am speaking of you raised to the level where you can make the same bold statement. Jesus' declaration that he was the fulfillment of scripture required a spiritual maturity of which most who heard his claim were not capable of understanding, but the purpose of life is to fulfill scripture.

Tonight, I will speak of conception which leads to scripture's fulfillment, as well as the shadow it casts in this world, for the same technique can be used to realize your objectives here.

There is only one Spirit. The Spirit of Man and the Spirit of God are the same. God's first great conception is recorded in the Old Testament as a foreshadowing of the event described in the first chapter of the Book of Luke, which tells the story of an angel of the Lord who speaks to Mary, saying: "Fear not, for you have found favor with God. You will conceive and bear a son and call his name Jesus." Wondering how this could be, since she had no husband, the angel explains the theory of supernatural conception, saying: "The Holy Spirit will come upon you and the power of the Most High will overshadow you; therefore the child to be born of you will be called holy, the Son of God." Now, the phrase, "come upon" and the word "overshadow" are the same by definition, and mean "superimposition; to be superimposed upon leaving your imprint, your seal."

In the 33rd chapter of the Book of Exodus, the Lord speaks to Moses, saying: "I will put you in a cleft of the rock and cover you with my hand, and when I have passed by I will remove my hand and you will see my back. You cannot see my glory, but you will see my back." This is the identical story of the angel and Mary. "I will put you in a cleft of the rock." In Hebrew the word "cleft" means "to bore; to penetrate; to pierce a quarry." And the phrase "I will cover you with my hands" means "copulation." Here is the creative act stated in the New Testament as: "The power of the Most High will overshadow you" for this act is "superimposition of oneself upon a being."

To illustrate my point let me share an experience of a friend who is here tonight. On the 5th day of March, just a few days ago, she said: "I found myself awake within a dream, sitting on a slab in a huge room, sterile and brilliantly lit. I knew it was a morgue, for I could see many girls to my right, each lying on a slab, appearing to be dead. A door opened and you, Neville, dressed as a physician and your nurse, a lady with very black hair, entered. As our eyes met I knew that you had had union with every one there, even though they appeared to be dead, and I also knew that I was next. Then a vivacious young girl entered the room and placed herself on a slab next to mine. Questioning her as to the whereabouts of your wife, I was told that she was sleeping in the next room. Upon hearing this, the nurse smiled and I recognized her as your wife, but wearing a wig. Embarrassed because of the knowledge of what was about to take place, I turned to the girl, who said: 'If you don't want him, I'll take him,' and with that the embarrassment turned to anger, and I said: 'Oh no! It is my turn.' Then union took place and I said to myself: 'He is like a stallion. How does he do it?' and the vision came to its end."

This vision has tremendous meaning, for God speaks to man in dream and reveals himself in vision. This was vision, for she was awake in the dream.

It is difficult for man to understand that God's creative power is personalized; that anyone raised from the dead and incorporated into the body of love is Jesus Christ, creating! In her vision everyone appeared to be dead, yet union had been consummated. All things are possible to God! By burying his creative power in them, he turns death into sleep and sleep into wakefulness and wakefulness into resurrection.

Now, those who slept on the marble slabs were as Moses on the rock. The world "cleft" used in this statement means "to bore; to pierce; to penetrate a quarry." God sends his creative power into this world of death to penetrate the dead. They will conceive and bear his child and call him Jesus. The words Jesus, Joshua, Jehovah all have the same root, which means "salvation." And if the child to be born of you will be called holy, the Son of God, then God must have fathered him. He cannot be the Son of God were he not fathered by God. People think that Man is not God, but I tell you that Man is all Imagination and Imagination is God. And when your Imagination is raised from this world in which it is buried, your creative power is used to impregnate the dead and bring them out as God.

It seems insane on a certain level, but I am telling you what I know from experience, and just as God impregnates the dead on a higher level, you can impregnate a dead state on this level. Think of a state and you are its spectator. And the state will remain dead relative to you until you penetrate it, until you approach it on your fiery chariot of imaginative power. An egg, whether it be human or that of a chicken, is dead and will remain so forever until the sperm penetrates it. The sperm must penetrate and occupy the egg in order to fertilize it, and then in its own given time the shell is broken and out comes that which was the sperm that penetrated it.

A state is penetrated through the act of assumption. Assuming you are now in the state you want to externalize, you think from it and no longer of it. Thinking from, you have penetrated the state. This penetration is still the mystery of all mysteries. Man has discovered how to go to the moon, place cameras in space, yet no matter what he knows concerning the mysteries of the universe, man cannot understand how an egg can be penetrated without a hole either before or after penetration. Well, your imagination is that sperm. You do not have to open doors to get into any room; you simply enter by assuming you are in it. Look at the world from it and feel what you want to feel, and the room has been penetrated. Now remain there until you feel relief. Of all the pleasures of the world, relief is the most keenly felt. So, when you enter into (penetrate) a desire, remain there until satisfaction is felt, until you have expelled the sperm right into the state.

The Lord told Moses he would cover him with his hand, which is his creative power. To cover is to copulate. Having covered you with his creative power, you are told that he removes it. In other words, you don't have to remain in that state. You are to go in and fertilize it, then remove your hand by returning your creative awareness to the former state.

Now it is said that you only see the back of God, but not his face. The lady who wrote the letter saw God's face, for she was awake. All of the others were apparently dead, totally unaware of what had happened to them; so, when the child is born it will come suddenly, as they will have no knowledge of conception. But they have conceived, because God never fails in his penetration, and they will all bring forth the child called the Son of God, as the symbol of their individual birth.

The lady who wrote the letter was awake when union took place, so she knows when it happened. I urge her to record this experience in her Bible next to the 35th verse of the 1st chapter of Luke. Mark it down: "On this day I conceived of the Holy Spirit." It will take thirty years! Should she drop dead now, it will not stop the conception. Rather she would find herself clothed in a body just like her present one - young, new, wonderful, with nothing missing, for she has not conceived physically, but in her soul. The soul is God's emanation, his wife 'til the sleep of death is past. That's where conception takes place, and from my own experience I say: birth will come about in thirty years. We are told Jesus began his ministry when he was about thirty years of age.

Everyone is fulfilling scripture, for everyone is Jesus Christ, he who comes only to fulfill what he foretold he would do. Taking upon himself the limitations of man (the limit of contraction and opacity) God fulfills scripture. It doesn't matter what the individual does for a living - whether he is a mason, a carpenter, a lawyer, a banker, a billionaire, or a pauper; the question is: is he fulfilling Scripture, for only as he fulfills scripture can he leave this world of death and enter the kingdom of heaven. God foretold what he was going to do, and then he became it. Scripture is the recordation of vision from beginning to end. It is not secular history. The characters recorded there did not live as you and I do. They are the personifications of states in which you and I, the immortal being called God, pass through as we fulfill scripture.

The story told in the 33rd chapter of Exodus is a foreshadowing of that which is fulfilled in the 1st chapter of the Book of Luke, as the angel explains the theory of spiritual or supernatural conception. In the Old Testament it is said: "I will cover you with my hand." If you take a good Hebrew dictionary you will discover this means copulation.

I know in my own case, when I stood in the presence of the Risen Lord, as we embraced we fused together. In the vision of this lady, everyone (save the physician) was female, so the fusing took place in a way that is normal for woman; but the union is not physical. Being the power of God, the image of God (which is the seed within him) is buried in the soul. Everyone appeared to be dead, and by this act God awakens the dead. We are urged to "Rise! Awake, O sleeper and rise from the dead." In this statement the dead and the sleeper are equated. In her vision the ladies were so asleep they seemed to be dead, but she knew union had taken place with all of them. This is the part the Risen Christ is sent to play. It does not take place on this level, for his energies are turned up into regeneration. The part he plays takes place in a remote area of the soul.

Now on the 20th of October, my friend Benny experienced the birth of the child. Last night Benny called to tell me that he saw David on the 6th day of March, the very day I foretold it would happen. He has promised to write the dream in detail to me, but this is what he told me over the phone: "In my dream I was invited to a party attended by many children and their parents. Suddenly the parents disappeared, leaving me alone with the children. As I looked around I noticed a lad about fourteen years of age walking toward me. Instantly I recognized him as David, and as I looked into his eyes I knew that he recognized me as his Father. Speaking directly to me, he said: 'I know our Father will never leave us.' Then the dream ended."

Here is the fulfillment of scripture. You see, God does not imitate, he does not repeat himself. In each case the same story is fulfilled, but is unique to the individual and never duplicated. Scripture says: "I go unto my Father and your Father, to my God and your God." Here is the plural: "Our Father will never leave us." The earthly fathers left, but the Spiritual Father will never leave us. Now I will prophesy for Benny. On the 8th day of July he will be split from top to bottom and ascend into heaven in serpentine form!

I tell you: we are only here to fulfill scripture. I don't care what you do in this world. If you sit in the White House tonight as the president of our great country you will exercise enormous power, but it would be as nothing compared to what you will experience when you have fulfilled scripture, and of this fulfillment you cannot fail! What can it matter what you accomplish in the outer world when you leave it all to go through the little gate called death? And no one knows the furnaces still to be experienced before the birth of the child!

But may I say to my friend who wrote the letter: you may depart this world in less than thirty years, but you will not falter. Benny is only about thirty years old now, so he has no memory of the conception; but no one can choose the time, for everyone is chosen. "You did not choose me, I chose you, for no man comes unto me save my Father calls him and I and my Father are one." No one can tell the secret of God's elective love, but when you are full of power, you are called. You don't volunteer, but are drafted, drawn into the state to reach its climax in thirty years!

To tell this to a vast audience would be the height of insanity, as they would not understand what I am talking about. But I tell you: your dreams, visions and experiences are symbols which you either accept and interpret or reject as an illusion, for there is nothing but God, who is your own wonderful human Imagination! There is only one Spirit in this wonderful universe. The being that maintains it all is the same being that maintains you! There is no other. "Man is all Imagination and God is Man and exists in us and we in him. The Eternal Body of Man is the Imagination and that is God Himself."[10]

And all things are possible to God! Just as an egg is penetrated, conceives, and is raised from the dead into a living state by bringing forth the express image of its person, if you bring forth the Son of God, you must have been fathered by God! My friend was awake within the dream, so she is aware of her marvelous conception. If she departs this section of time before the thirty years it will make no difference, for unlike the children here, where a miscarriage is possible, she cannot lose the child!

I have read books on sex symbolism in the Bible where these great scholars consider this passage in Luke to be pornography. If you read it on that level you will see God as a creator, creating. Every child born of woman is God creating, for he is the creator of all. But when he calls you from above, your energies are reversed and spring from above, while the energies of this world spring from below, so you move from generation to regeneration.

Now let me come back to this level and show you how to go about realizing your objectives. What you want, be it health, wealth, or fame, is only a state. Think of the state as an egg containing everything necessary to externalize itself, but dead and must be penetrated and fertilized in order to break the shell and become what the world calls reality. Let me illustrate. As I stand here before you, I desire and will assume that I am in San Francisco, approximately 500 miles from here. (I think I know this city well, but I don't have to know a city in order to assume a state.) Putting myself in a familiar hotel lobby, I sit there and think of the world relative to the lobby in which I am now seated. While I am here I feel its reality; I feel the satisfaction of being here, the very place I wanted to be. The moment I feel the relief of being here, I have released the necessary sperm, or

---

[10] William Blake

energy, into that dead state. Then I return to Los Angeles, but in that short period of time I have gone and prepared the experience. Now I will move across a bridge of events which will compel me to go to San Francisco. I may have no desire to go, but I will; for I have prepared the place, occupied it, and although I returned to where I was and later may resist the going, I cannot stop it, for I have created it and I will fulfill what I have done.

Now you can do this with everything. An objective, a desire, is an egg, which you can penetrate and occupy. You can move right into it and view the world from it. Don't think of it; view the world from it, which implies that you are in it. Then feel the relief, the satisfaction, of being there. Do this and no power in the world can stop you from realizing that state. You may regret what you did, but you will fulfill it anyway. Learn your lesson and try not to do that which you do not want to experience in the future.

Everything is waiting for you to penetrate, as everything is in the cleft rock. Your desire is just as dead as a rock, so you penetrate it by going right into it, occupying, and viewing the world from it. Then, feeling the relief of being in it and the satisfaction of accomplishment, turn your back on it knowing you have done it, and allow it to objectify itself in your world.

That is a creative act on this level, just as my friend saw the creative act on another level. It frightens people just to think of this, because our moralists have the strangest concept of God. When two people love each other deeply and that love is consummated, is that something apart from God when God is love? I wish everyone would read Blake and see what he thinks of the so-called moral virtues, of those who distort the vision of Jerusalem, this wonderful being of liberty.

Tonight, know what you want and go right in and occupy it. Don't ask anyone's permission; just put yourself into the state you desire to experience by asking yourself this question: "How would I feel if I saw the world from that state?" Do you know you can put yourself into any state? My son actually put himself into the state of war by reading a book about Guadalcanal and falling in love with the pictures of the natives there! He certainly didn't enjoy his experiences while there, but he asked for it. You see: nothing happens by accident. Everything that happens in the world does so because you and I set them in motion, whether we do it wittingly or unwittingly.

Again, I wanted to share my thrill with all of you in Benny's wonderful experience of seeing David, and this lady's vision of being sired. I promise her it will take thirty years - but what is thirty years in eternity? What is thirty years when you bring forth the Christ child? May everyone have it! God doesn't have just one stallion; he has a wonderful stable full of those who are the resurrected Christ, those whose power has been raised from the dead and turned around from generation to regeneration. He selects those who are to be saved and sends them, under command to play the part of the creative power of God.

Believe me, God is Man. "Thou art a Man, God is no more. Thine own Humanity, learn to adore." Everything is Man. About 4:00 o'clock this morning I saw a six-story, stark white building in vision, and as I looked at it, it became a Man. It took on the human face. All the mountains, rivers, valleys -everything is Man, and when you are awake you commune with them as friends. You walk into all the areas of the world to discover that everything is God and God is Man.

Now let us go into the silence.

Also Available From This Publisher

All Things Are Possible
ISBN 978-1-60386-740-5

Invisible Helpers
ISBN 978-1-60386-741-2

A Divine Event and Other Essays
ISBN 978-1-60386-742-9

An Assured Understanding & Other Sermons
ISBN 978-1-60386-743-6

Behold the Dreamer Cometh
ISBN 978-1-60386-744-3

Christ in You
ISBN 978-1-60386-722-1

The Way to the Kingdom
ISBN 978-1-60386-720-7

The Way Out
ISBN 978-1-60386-715-3

The Necessity of Prayer
ISBN 978-1-60386-714-6

Christ in You
ISBN 978-1-60386-710-8

The Golden Key & 22 Essays
ISBN 978-1-60386-706-1

At Your Command
ISBN 978-1-60386-677-4

You Can Never Outgrow I Am
ISBN 978-1-60386-676-7

Neville Goddard: The Essential Collection
978-1-60386-678-1

www.ingramcontent.com/pod-product-compliance
Lightning Source LLC
Chambersburg PA
CBHW020558030426
42337CB00013B/1139